WITH SACRED THREADS

WITH SACRED THREADS

Quilting and the Spiritual Life

Susan Towner-Larsen and Barbara Brewer Davis

United Church Press

Cleveland, Ohio

United Church Press, Cleveland, Ohio 44115

www.ucpress.com

Grateful acknowledgment for permission to reprint the following: From *North Carolina Quilts*, edited by Ruth Haislip Roberson. Copyright © 1988 by the University of North Carolina Press. Used by permission of the publisher. ▪ From *A Communion of the Spirits: African-American Quilters, Preservers, and Their Stories* by Roland L. Freeman, copyright 1996, and reprinted by permission of Rutledge Hill Press, Nashville, Tennessee. ▪ From John and Poakalani Serrao, *The Hawaiian Quilt: A Spiritual Experience*. Reprinted by permission. ▪ From Laurie Bushbaum, "Woman of the Cloth," *Art Quilt Magazine*, issue 9 (1998). Reprinted by permission.

Biblical quotations, unless otherwise noted, are from the New Revised Standard Version of the Bible, © 1989 by the Division of Christian Education of the National Council of Churches of Christ in the U.S.A., and are used by permission. Adaptations have been made for inclusivity.

Printed in the United States of America on acid-free paper

05   04   03   02   01   00   5   4   3   2   1

Library of Congress Cataloging-in-Publication Data

Towner-Larsen, Susan, 1950–
    With sacred threads : quilting and the spiritual life / Susan Towner-Larsen and
Barbara Brewer Davis.
      p. cm.
    Includes bibliographical references.
    ISBN 0-8298-1384-5 (pbk. : alk. paper)
    1. Quiltmakers—Prayer-books and devotions—English.   2. Quilts—United States.
I. Davis, Barbara Brewer, 1943–   II. Title.

BV4596.N44 .T69 2000
242'.68—dc21   00-042317

CONTENTS

To my mom, who taught me to love and to quilt,

To my daughters, Kara and Krista, whom I love more than words or even quilts can say,

To Barb, good friend, can we quilt now?

And to Bob, who "oohs and ahs" at all the right moments,

Thanks, dear ones! I do love you.

—S. T.-L.

To Terry, my best and most enthusiastic champion
of all my explorations, who continues to smile anyway.

To Jamie and Greg and Leah, my children, who each in his or her own way
has taught me a great deal about really being alive and what risking love means.

To my sister, Scottie, who has long been a mentor for me.

And to my parents, who continue to be tremendous examples of how and where
to find the creative and spiritual connections in every day.

"Yes, Susan, let's quilt now!"

—B. B. D.

FOREWORD

quilt is "earthly mysticism." It dares to venture into the mystery, to dance at the edge of the unknown, fathom the deep things, perchance God. Where language falls mute, where reason has produced its last halting step toward truth, the arts begin, among them, now, quilting. Yet it is firmly grounded, rooted in the routine of the needle and thread of color and texture, of eye and hand.

A quilter is a "psalmist." When you can't merely say it, when words fail, you sing it, dance it . . . quilt it. Joy or sadness, hope or despair, peace or anger, love or hate. Forthright, courageous, unapologetic. Boisterous and vivid, shy and muted. Halting and hesitant, persistent and bold. Gift *from* a psalmist, yet just as often gift *to* the psalmist. Cathartic. Cleansing. Renewing. A vigorous dance with the Divine. Wrestling. Contesting. Intimate. Life-giving.

A quilt is a "hologram." Multi-dimensional in time and space. It reaches *downward*, into and out from the one who dares to cut and position, sew and cushion. It probes the depth, opens the heart, unmasks and unveils. Even as it reaches *outward*, a quilt so often a gift of community, quilters working their own piece side-by-side or working the same piece together. It reaches inevitably *upward*, toward the Heart of the Sacred. A quilt *faces forward*, looking outward toward a viewer to tell its story. Yet it oddly *faces backward* at the same time, its story emerging from behind it, or beneath it. How far back in time does it reach? How many years, decades, even centuries—from the earlier forming of the oldest fragment—does it stretch? For every inch of visibility, it reveals vast dimensions of invisibility. For all that may be known about it, its echoes of the unknown reverberate. How many races, ethnic groups, religions, classes, life situations whisper from its collage of shape and color? What *tones* of voice sing from it? Struggle, toil, laughter, anguish, shouts, whispers. Across the full range of human emotion.

A quilt is "meaning-seeking." Brother David Steindl-Rast, a contemplative monk, for whom English is a second language, points out how often we use "purpose" and "meaning" as if they were synonyms. A quilt can be *purposeful*—the artistic expression of an intent of the quilter. Conveying a message already discerned. A quilt already seen in a mind's eye, sketched on a pad, a pattern to replicate onto the frame. *Purpose* suggests clarity, intent, effort. But a quilt is also *meaning-seeking*— open, receptive, hospitable to the gift of meaning that will come amidst the work. *Meaning-seeking* is mindfully passive, quietly poised, alert and watchful. Perhaps quilt art awaits and awakens the muse of the fabric, the moment when thread and fabric, indeed, become art. At a writer's workshop one author shared his discipline of writing: "At eight o'clock each morning I sharpen my pencils, open my pad, and begin to write." The discipline of the art intentional and purposeful. But another suggested: "When the music visits, day or night, I stop whatever I am doing, take pen in hand, and dare to capture the gift." The gift of art. Receptive to the mystery of meaning.

Rev. Dr. Howard E. Friend Jr.

Recovering the Sacred Center

ACKNOWLEDGMENTS

s in the germination of any idea, this book has its roots in fertile soil. Both of us have been fed and nurtured by stories of all those who came before us as creative women. We have also been encouraged and spurred on to pursue this project about quilting and spirituality by those who have already discovered this and who now live out this connection. We are deeply grateful to the people who took the time to answer our questionnaire or, in one form or another, have been willing to share their stories with us. These sacred sharings are often "intimate" stories of their connection with their Creator and of their very unique discoveries about both the process of quilting and their spiritual journeys. For this, we extend our heartfelt thanks for "putting it out there" and for being willing to share their most profound understanding of how the Holy is present to their work and play.

We also thank our publisher and especially Kim Sadler, the editor of United Church Press, for having faith in our ability to put this information into some form that not only makes sense but, we hope, will touch the lives of our readers.

Many friends and colleagues were very helpful in directing us to appropriate sources. We thank Ann Bowers, an English professor at Ohio State University who put us onto the wonderful videotape *Unraveling the Stories* about Ohio quilt makers. Howard and Betsy Friend have offered unlimited time and suggestions about spiritual connections and creativity, and Karen Roller gave generously of her very busy life to proof and edit our manuscript and to enthusiastically urge us onward. At every turn new people were willing to share their art, their resources, and their referrals, making this endeavor a delightfully communal adventure.

Last, but certainly not least, we thank our families. They gave up their precious time at the computer screens and E-mail in deference to our deadlines. We value most the love and support that were always there as we explored new edges in our own frontiers as writers and creative women, especially from our spouses, Terry and Bob, and our children.

And God, thanks!

INTRODUCTION

ur passion for quilting and its striking connection to our spiritual lives would not let go of us. We would sit together, working on quilts, glorious fabrics spread everywhere, two sewing machines humming intermittently, teacups in varying stages of needing to be refilled, and time would stand still. Our conversations and reflections ran deep, immersing us in a sense of awe. Unfolding before us was the work of our hands. Unfolding within us was the reality of the sacred connectedness of quilting and spirituality. We had come together to quilt. Yet we found ourselves hungering in common for glimpses of the Holy, and we were amazed when those glimpses appeared at our fingertips.

The subject of spirituality is popular these days. Certainly, for two women at the midpoint of our lives—

when little seems settled or permanent—our understanding of spirituality continues to emerge. What quilt making helped crystallize for us, however, is what we came to recognize as the essence of spirituality—the connecting of our daily life experiences with our experiences of God. We find God is in the everydayness of our lives. Whatever we do that draws us closer to God and enables us to listen more deeply for the Holy, that is a connection to the sacred. Some everyday occurrences, routines, or practices consistently open us to those connections between the everyday and the sacred. For some people, the connections come most often through nature; for some, through prayer or through children; for others, through silence or through reading. The possibilities are limitless. For us, quilting is one of those trusted connectors.

Thread is essential for quilting and is also a symbol of connectedness. Many threads are woven together into cloth, and typically, many different fabrics are used in one quilt. When we piece together the fabrics, we use yards and yards of thread, and we cut that thread countless times. We sew one piece of fabric to another, then cut away the excess thread. No backstitching or knotting motion is used in piecing a quilt as is done in the sewing of a clothing garment. Instead, in a quilt each new seam covers the unknotted end of the last seam, making every piece and every seam secure and a part of the whole. Many small sections of fabric and thread, then, eventually come together into one piece, one continuous thread, one quilt. Each section of thread or piece of fabric is essential to the whole. Thread became for us a reminder of individual sacredness and of the many incredible ways that we are all woven together into the fabric of life.

When we first started quilting together, we decided to save even the many excess, cut-away pieces of thread. We put them in a basket, gathering them through the seasons, waiting for spring when the birds might use them for nests. These threads, too, remind us that even what we might typically discard from our lives—

the pains and hurts and parts of ourselves we like the least—may eventually be transformed into something new, some new piece of the life cycle.

All moments of life are pieces of the sacred whole of our being. In our experience, God does not usually rush in to fix our deep wounds or rescue us from life's pains. Rather, God stands with us in some mysterious way, gathering us to God's self. In an amazing grace-filled fashion, over time, God enables us to weave together the seemingly loose and unconnected threads of our lives into moments of sacred wholeness.

Quilting is not unique in its capacity to bind the sacred and the everyday. Like other disciplines or practices or artistic expressions, quilting is rich in both symbolism and traditions. Quilting is rich, too, in opportunities that open us to experiences of God. The spiritual journey is a journey inward as well as outward, sometimes returning us to places of great woundedness and sometimes opening us to fresh experiences of awe and wonder.

We need all the encouragement and support we can get along the way! Quilting is one of the contexts for "going deep and surfacing," for finding the sacred challenge and support on the journey toward God and self.

This book is an attempt to reflect on the endless ways that quilting is a context for the spiritual journey. Each chapter centers on a theme that connects to life in the Spirit and to life as a quilter. The metaphors and stories that thread their way through these two overlapping worlds demonstrate emphatically that the sacred exists in the routine happenings of our lives. With thread in hand, we found we were able to bridge generations and remember our heritage and hopes. Immersed in the many textures of cloth, we explored the content of our souls, the nature of our God, and the needs of our world. Often exhilarated, sometimes weary, we were not alone on this journey. Coinciding with the unfolding of our quilting passion, we enrolled together in Wellstreams, a training program for spiritual directors. Family and friends, teachers, other students, our spiritual directors, and many quilters of our acquaintance inspired us and endured us along the way. The themes and connections that were touching us seemed to resonate with others as well.

Each chapter begins with "Threads of Tradition," where we share one of the many legacies or practices related to quilting. In "Threads of Our Souls" we present the reflections and stories that tie the tradition to the spiritual journey. At the end of each chapter, "Threads of Reflection" offers a photograph of a quilt for contemplation and the possibility of connecting our stories to the stories and experiences of the reader.

"Quilts have always told visual stories, been a celebration of living and surviving, spoken for those without voices, and recorded for posterity important events in their makers' lives."[1] May the quilts and impressions shared in these pages empower your voice and inspire the discovery of sacred connections in your life stories.

· ART ·

And around the throne is a rainbow that looks like an emerald.

—Revelation 4:36

THREADS OF TRADITION

There is a saying about quilts attributed to the early days of their history in this country: "We made them fast to keep our families warm and we made them beautiful so our hearts wouldn't break." Who might have spoken such powerful truth? Pioneer women, slave women, immigrant men and women, people of many walks of life and from various countries made quilts for their families' survival and contributed to the early history of this art form. Any of them might have uttered those moving words. Although the process of quilt making slowed and became

1

less urgent as our country matured, the necessity for quilts and the power of their presence in women's lives remained intact. That incredible ability to "keep our hearts from breaking" draws women and men into quilt making even today, inviting us to express many of our innermost passions and compassion. Within the threads of our quilts are stitched the stories of our souls and of our country's soul. The joys and sorrows of many lifetimes are captured without words in the legacy of our nation's quilted artwork.

For a while after World War II, quilt making in the United States lost some of its popularity. With more women in the workforce, more manufactured goods, and most homes with central heating, quilt making for European American women persisted largely in the form of a leisurely, enjoyable pastime. Later in that era, however, a different perspective began to emerge. Kathlyn Fender Sullivan writes of that time: "The realization began to grow that quilts are a true and valid art form, both functional and decorative, based on an artistic development unique to our country. Coupled with this came a new recognition of the American woman's innate and continuous creativity. Today quilting is assuming its rightful place in both our cultural heritage and the ongoing evolution of the arts."[1]

Meanwhile, African American quilters had gone largely unnoticed and unrecognized. Their sense of isolation from each other and the lack of artistic recognition of their work persisted for many years. In the early years of documenting quilts, some scholars incorrectly identified a certain style of African American quilting as "authentic," leaving the larger body of African American quilts and quilters unrecognized. To counter their sense of isolation, Carolyn Mazloomi, quilt artist and quilt historian, formed the national organization Women of Color Quilt Network in 1986. Six years later, in 1992, Cuesta Benberry revolutionized the world of quilting with the research to validate and an exhibit to demonstrate the wide variety of styles and talents of African American quilters. With the support and encouragement of these key women, the spirit and appreciation of African American quilts soared. Today, Dr. Mazloomi's book *Spirits of the Cloth: Contemporary African-American Quilts* beautifully immortalizes the depth of spirit and the vast range of talent of women of color.

THREADS OF OUR SOULS

Linking art, imagination, and spiritual growth is not new. Icons, hymns, sculptures, paintings, weavings, beadwork, carvings—and many other forms of artistic expression—have long been valued for their ability to take us into the Holy; to reveal some deeper knowledge of ourselves or our God; to express some insight; to illuminate, challenge, clarify, or puzzle; or to stir our hearts to soaring wonderment. Often without words, artists help us express something or experience something anew.

"The arts have an especially great power to represent not only the ordinary in our experience and faith, but the very deepest aspects of it."[2] Quilts represent our everyday lives: our need for warmth and beauty, and our need for creative expression. They arise out of our daily juggling of time and commitments and priorities. They express the moods and the colors and the designs of life's joys, pains, and realities. And they take us deeper. Quilts call us to memories and to remembering. With memories, there is always "more," more to reflect upon, more ways to reenter an experience, more insight into the lifelong process of coming to wholeness, to our own true selves. Often autobiographical, quilts inspire us and challenge us to read and value our own stories, the stories of generations before and after us. Also, quilts call us to hope, to look to the future, and to claim our deeply held convictions about the sanctity of life and our unshakable aspirations for humankind.

Many stories that we have been privileged to receive from quilters acknowledge the power of quilting's artistic expression. Whether it is in dancing around the design table or being overwhelmed by a sense of the Spirit while sewing, whether it is delight in the colors and designs of fabric or the healing quality of engaging in the artful expression of one's feelings—quilting is an art form that grows out of our everyday lives, that helps us discern meaning out of our experiences, and that challenges us to find the Sacred in the very midst of the creative process.

Imaginative women and men from around the world have embraced quilting's artistic potential and have stretched the art to great and diverse heights. Reflecting the essence of the artist, quilts also are invested with the stories, meanings, and traditions of the culture from which they arise. African American quilters frequently employ symbols, cloth, and colors from their African heritage. The unique and beautiful Hawaiian quilts are another illustration of this art form's versatility:

> The missionary women taught the Hawaiian women how to make quilts, but the Hawaiian women saw no meaning in patchwork quilts. The patchwork quilts had no stories or traditions they could relate to. The Hawaiian women therefore gave the quilts a meaning and a purpose for themselves. They placed all of their traditional designs into the quilt and made their own unique form of quilting—The Hawaiian Quilt. . . . Every stitch had meaning and every part of the design had a purpose. Hawaiian quilting became an art form. Hawaiian quilting became the very essence of being Hawaiian.[3]

Hmong women of Cambodia and the Kuna Indian women of the Caribbean also developed unique processes for appliqué and quilting. Their *pa ndau* designs (Hmong) and *molas* (Kuna Indian) adorn clothing, wall hangings, and quilts seen worldwide.

One cannot ponder quilt making without calling to mind the beautiful and unique quilts of Amish women. With their vibrant, rich colors and countless variations on traditional designs, the quilts of Amish women have inspired many others to become quilters. Sue Bender, author of *Plain and Simple,* was one of those women. Her inspiration took her even farther, into a rare opportunity to live within an Amish household. Of the Amish view of quilting and of art, Sue wrote:

> The concept of art did not exist; in their world every woman quilted and made dolls for her children. There was no reason to single out anyone and label her an artist. . . . The mother's ego didn't have to compete with the object: the utility of the object, not the reflection of the maker, was what was important. . . . Strength was based on necessity. Beauty came by chance. I learned about art . . . from these people who didn't have the word "artist" in their vocabulary. I looked at their life and saw it as art.[4]

"Quilting is memory's art."[5] Concerned about the memories and legacies of their island, John and Poakalani Serrao design and document the art and traditions of the Hawaiian quilt. In their book *The Hawaiian Quilt: A Spiritual Experience,* John writes,

> Recording and documenting one's life history is very important, and what a beautiful way to express it but on a Hawaiian Quilt. My greatest joy is seeing one of my designs develop from an idea or inspiration onto a paper pattern and then into a beautiful quilt. It is breathtaking to see the quilt designs forever documenting the life and times of the quilter. It gives me a feeling of accomplishment to know that as a cultural artist I am helping to pass on the legacy and history of our families and Hawaii.[6]

Other quilters described for us their artistic process and sense of legacy. Jinny Smanik of Connecticut said:

I find that cloth "speaks" to me. The colors and shapes evoke emotions, and the creation of quilts allows me to express myself in a way that I was not able to prior to quilting. I have always considered myself to have had an artistic "eye" for color and design. I have been blessed with an appreciation of the beauty of God's world and have sought to find a way to give back some of that beauty that I see. I'm not a painter . . . I cannot draw, but I can sew. I can put together quilts that speak from my heart, and hopefully to the hearts of others.

In Ohio, Suzanne Evenson told us:

Most of my works have stories behind them. As I begin a new piece, I do sketchy drawings. Starting from a concept or working title, I initiate a dialogue with myself about these ideas. I begin the construction process by selecting materials, allowing the interplay of color, pattern and texture to guide the early phases of the process. Working intuitively, I allow myself to place colors and shapes that express my mood and often the original sketches and materials are replaced by others. The stories and the art emerge simultaneously.

Two of Suzanne's art quilts are included in this book on pages 24 and 80.

Vikki Pignatelli, a quilt artist and the creator of "The Fire Within" on page 32, wrote these words about the deeply Spirit-filled and emotional process of creating that quilt:

Making this quilt was a paradox for me, feeling at the same time both joyous and afraid. Joyous because I was given a creative talent and chosen to make this artwork. And the Spirit was helping me! Terrified because that defies our human logic. Am I imagining things? Why pick me when there are others far more gifted? Who could I tell? Who would believe me? Yet, I know what I sensed. My only answer is that I was willing to do the work.

As Vikki describes so well, artists in many mediums are frequently aware of being inspired by and expressive of something larger than themselves, something sacred and beyond the ordinary. Experience teaches us that such is the nature of quilting, and wisdom reveals that such is the nature of the Holy.

"In Paradisuum II" by Linda Fowler, photographed by Kevin Fitzsimmons.
Created in memoriam for a friend, based on Faure's symphony of this title.

THREADS OF REFLECTION

Centering Prayer

Affirm within me, God, the artist you inspire me to be.

Scripture

God saw everything that God had made, and indeed, it was very good.
—Genesis 1:31

Quilt Reflections

Enjoy and ponder the quilt pictured on page 8.

Linda Fowler, internationally known quilt artist, created this quilt in memory of a priest friend who had died. The design is based on her friend's favorite musical piece.

What features on the quilt stand out for you?

What is your favorite song or piece of music?

If you were to create a quilt based on that music, what colors and designs would you include?

What feelings, heritage, or experiences would your quilt express?

In your journal, or on a piece of paper, sketch your quilt. What would you tell others about it?

What is your experience of being an artist?

How might you nurture the artist within you?

Prayer

Creator, Artist God,

Your artwork is all around me. For the beauty of creation, I thank you. Be with me in moments when I fail to claim my own creative talents. Inspire my imagination with an inner well of images, colors, stories, and designs that nourish my soul. Inspire, too, my expression of those images and stories in ways I may not have considered before. Amen.

STORYTELLING

THREADS OF TRADITION

Narrative quilts literally tell stories and document historical events. Peggie Hartwell shares her legacy as a pictorial quilter:

> I had the good fortune to live in a household of extended family members, where some of the men were great storytellers. Among them, however, was one master storyteller . . . this was my grandfather, William Tyler, Sr. His stories were so passionate—so alive—he all but sang them like living epics. As I sat at his feet soaking up his every word, I had no

idea that he was leaving me a legacy of storytelling. The only difference between us is that my grandfather told his stories in the oral tradition and I now tell mine through pictorial quilts. Narrative quiltmaking has become my voice in cloth.[1]

One pictorial quilt done in the late 1990s tells the story of how African Americans escaped to freedom by way of the Underground Railroad. Barbara Payne, who lives in Ohio, has designed and pieced a narrative quilt that shares several of the important aspects and symbols woven within the stories of the Underground Railroad that was in operation in the mid-nineteenth century. (See the chapter "Liberation" for further details about the Railroad.)

Barbara was not taught about the Underground Railroad in her schooling in Georgia. She decided to educate herself about this significant piece of her own ancestors' heritage. She first went to the public library to ask for reference material and was referred to the "train" section of the library. She then realized it was also important to educate the public about the legacy of the Underground Railroad. Barbara designed and created the quilt on page 16. Her quilt is indeed a fabric storyteller or "griot" out of the African tradition. This colorful work, with eighteen panels of "secret signs," related to the manner in which slaves escaped from plantations where they had been held in servitude. They found their way to freedom in the northern United States and Canada, aided by encoded messages in spirituals, quilts, and secret information passed on by the "conductors" of the Railroad. The lively legend of Barbara's quilt is as follows:

- A young slave woman with her infant "backed up to the wall" as she searches in the rain in hopes of freedom. Barbara says, "The woman is praying. That is all we can do when we are backed up against the wall."

- Stars. They "gave light and guided the fugitives during the night."
- Harriet Tubman. She "was called the 'Moses' of the Underground Railroad because she helped more than three hundred slaves to escape to freedom."
- A decoy wagon. "Wagons were filled with vegetables, wood, hay or manure and the underneath, inside of the wagon was used to hide the fugitives in a secret compartment."
- Musical notes. "The slaves communicated by song and music."
- The faithful groomsman. "An iron painted black man holding a lit lantern signaled a safe place for fugitives."
- Quilts. They were "used for warmth and hiding while traveling."
- The drinking gourd. It "was the name given to the Big Dipper by slaves as the handle was used as a guide to the North Star."
- African American spirituals. These "signaled to slaves that it was time to 'wave in the water' or travel by water so as to lose the scent of their trail and confuse slave catchers."
- House. "A Quaker abolitionist home was used to provide safety until the fugitives could move on to the next 'station.'"
- Hands. "Black and white hands worked together in unity in the struggle for freedom."
- Red roses. "Each rose in a vase indicated the number of fugitives hiding within a home or station."
- Black pots. "If a pot was turned upside down it was not safe to enter and if the pot was sitting right side up it meant that it was a safe home or safe place."

Barbara Payne's quilt is now moving from school to school as a critical piece of African American history curriculum. The quilt has also traveled to many foreign lands, and as she says, "It has seen many more places than I have!"

Dr. Carolyn Mazloomi, an art quilter, shares, "I love quilts that tell stories about our lives. I like to think of these quilts as historical documents. People will look at these quilts and get a glimpse at how we led our lives and what is happening socially and politically not only for us but those around us."[2]

THREADS OF OUR SOULS

As Deena Metzger states, "Stories both house the soul and are the process through which we make soul. . . . By becoming aware of our stories and their complexities, we access soul because through story, we make meaning."[3]

Storytellers were revered in oral cultures that relied exclusively upon these persons for the safekeeping and transmission of their spiritual and cultural heritage. The listeners of the story engaged their entire selves (body and soul) in the process of gathering in the essence of the story. There was an embodied nature to these stories as they literally carried the message of meaning-making for indigenous groups. In African cultures the griot was the "community storyteller and keeper of cultural heritage, history, and stories."[4] The wise older woman or crone in a Latino village, the Hindi guru, the Buddhist Zen master, and the elders of American Indian traditions were (and still are) seen as carriers of great wisdom.

In a recent visit to Taos Pueblo, the oldest continuously active native peoples' pueblo in New Mexico, we learned that the storyteller is depicted as a woman with children climbing on her, sitting at her feet, and listening with great intent to her wisdom. The storyteller is very approachable and loving, and encourages the children to listen and hear the wisdom of their elders. The storyteller symbol is found in jewelry, pottery, and painting. This symbol is among the most prized in Taos Pueblo, as it is among other southwestern native peoples.

Hebrews and early Christians lived in oral cultures. The stories that now make up our sacred texts are the carriers of wisdom and narrative that made meaning for those Middle Eastern groups. Once the stories were recorded, they became the foundation for our Judeo-Christian faith. The Hebrew and Christian Scriptures continue to be holy texts for modern-day people of faith. The stories continue to inspire, perplex, and challenge those who study these texts today.

Biblical stories carry an elemental understanding of connections with the Holy. They encourage us to move into a one-on-one relationship with God, something that writers of the Hebrew and Christian Scriptures seemed to comprehend and to live. Jesus was the quintessential storyteller, surprising us with parables that called for immersion in story to make meaning.

Joseph Campbell pointed out in an interview with Bill Moyers that "what we are seeking is an experience of being alive, so that our life experience on the purely physical plane will have resonance within our own innermost being and reality."[5] We struggle today with ways of capturing this sense of being alive. Without readily identifiable storytellers, we search for ways to integrate what we know with how we live.

At the dawning of the twenty-first century we are in danger of losing the value of story. We sit in front of a cold computer screen, removed from community and a context within which to hear the story. There is no sensory prompter that stimulates expansion of our imagination. It is far too easy to just gather the words and numbly watch images drift across the screen. Stories disembodied, without a live or tactile storyteller of some kind, seem disposable and without connection to any meaning for us—without "soul."

Perhaps this is one reason that quilting is experiencing such a resurgence in our country, especially in European American and African American homes. *Quilters Newsletter* reported that there is a quilter in 12.2 percent of all U.S. households, with more than 650,000 dedicated quilters nationwide. These people average 13.6 projects per year, or more than forty-two hours each month on their quilting projects.[6]

Quilts embody stories. The process of bringing a quilt to life—of birthing its story—is one of engagement and commitment, often taking a long time to complete. This gestation allows the quilt maker long periods of reflection and participation in the process of meaning-making with the cloth before her. This meaning-making happens within the context of community where storytelling is a part of the process of crafting the final legend.

Lou Jane Gatford of Milwaukee was proud to be invited at age seven into her grandmother's quilting circle. The older women in that group taught her how to make precise stitching (ten to twelve inches being the best quilting), and she was thrilled to be considered accurate enough to be accepted in the group of "experts." However, she says that the best part of that summer around the quilting table was "hearing everyone's story." Her grandmother "had traveled in wagon trains and 'proved up' on three homesteads herself in Missouri, Oklahoma, and the Cherokee Strip. Most of the women in this quilting group were immigrants who had struggled through the Depression and the Dust Bowl. Most of the women had been home-steaders, immigrants, indentured servants, etc." Sharing their stories as they quilted kept these memories alive: "The common thread between these women was a love of God, perseverance, and graceful maturing." These women gave Lou Jane her sense of meaning and imparted important values to her as they stitched.

Today, cloth continues to tell stories. Daphne Taylor, a quilt artist in Maine, discovered a stash of fabric at a garage sale. As Daphne negotiated with its owner for a bargain, she could appreciate that "these bits of cloth were one woman's life [story]. I remember bartering with her [for the stash]. I could see the woman's lips moving slightly as she gave up this bag of memories. Textiles do tell stories; they refresh our memories."[7] One wonders, With whom did this woman share these stories?

"Underground Railroad Secret Signs" by Barbara Payne.
Designed and quilted to honor and teach about this important
aspect of African American history.

THREADS OF REFLECTION

Centering Prayer

Hum or sing this familiar hymn to yourself: "I love to tell the story, because I know 'tis true."

Scripture

Keep these words that I am commanding you today in your heart. Recite them to your children and talk about them when you are at home and when you are away, when you lie down and when you rise.

—Deuteronomy 6:6–7

Quilt Reflections

What stories from your life, your spiritual or religious traditions, encircle you? How have they drawn you closer to God? to your neighbor?

Ponder the quilt on page 16. If you were designing a story quilt about your own life, what stories and symbols would you use?

Prayer

I thank you, Creator of All Stories, for the connections with my ancestors and their life experiences. I thank you for the creative ways you provide for us to share all stories and preserve them for future generations. As I go about this soul-work, help me to make meaning and connections that bring me back home to you.

FINDING OUR VOICES

There is no speech, nor are there words;
their voice is not heard;
yet their voice goes out through all the earth,
and their words to the end of the world.

—Psalm 19:3–4

THREADS OF TRADITION

The voices of women quilters come through loud and clear in their art. It has always been so. Whenever and wherever cultures or societies suppressed women's expression of themselves or their use of their own "voices," quilts and other crafts became their creative outlet. Whenever voice and power were stolen from women, the creative, expressive process of quilt making snatched both back.

Crazy quilts, extremely popular during the last twenty years of the nineteenth century, reflected a "quiet protest"[1] on the part of women.

> The hallmark of the crazy quilt was its lack of structure, and women pushed that attribute to the limit. . . . In retrospect the crazy quilt may not seem much of a revolution for women, but it was a beginning. Women had learned from painful experience the value of patience and the safety of silence. Our sisters of a century ago lacked the platforms for protest that we enjoy today, but they had their domestic arts. . . . The crazy quilts that warmed their beds and decorated their parlors reflect what was in their hearts. Subconsciously at least, women pieced together manifestos that rejected the neat little geometric compartments of daughter, housewife, and mother. The cloth angles, the random strips, the odd-sized pieces, all had this message. The colors in crazy quilts also tend to rage, one against another, and the arrangement of pieces takes on the appearance of scraps dropped heedlessly to the floor—a silent rebellion against the status quo.[2]

Snatching back voice and power, African American quilters embody their struggle for liberation in their art as well. In *Spirits of the Cloth: Contemporary African-American Quilts*, quilter Cathleen R. Bailey says,

> I had no quilting experience, so I read books and watched TV quilt shows, where white women taught me never to use too much yellow, and that red could be overpowering. I felt constricted. Then, in a dream, my ex-slave great-grandmother Margaret appeared and admonished

me. "Throw all the colors together," she said. "They'll go. Won't they?" All the colors *do* go together. Thank you, women in my family. I'm loosened. I'm a smiling quilter.[3]

THREADS OF OUR SOULS

It is a struggle to take back our voices, reclaim what we know, and speak our own lives. Connections and relationships are important to women. We spend a lot of our time sorting them out, observing how they work or don't work, striving to build better connections to others and to ourselves. The irony is that our experience teaches us from early on in life that to speak what is on our minds or in our hearts—to give voice to all of the feelings, questions, concerns, joys, and struggles—frequently drives people away or strains our connections to them. We lose community, relationships, and a sense of belonging. Yet when we learn to filter those truths, to temper what we say because of what others do not want to hear, we connect deeply to no one. The profound sorrow for many of us is that in the censoring process, we also lose our connection with ourselves; we stop listening to the inner voice and stop trusting our feelings and wisdom.

In their book *Daughters of the Moon, Sisters of the Sun,* authors K. Wind Hughes and Linda Wolf relate the experience of beginning the Girls Focus Group in order to listen to, understand, and connect to girls today. "One of the biggest obstacles in the beginning was when we asked girls what they felt. They would answer, 'I don't know.' We responded, 'Girls, you do know and we'll sit here as long as you need to, until you are quiet enough to listen deeply within yourself and it will come.'"[4] What wisdom and caring in that response! Once the "permission to go deeper, beyond self-doubt" was given, "the floodgates opened and we discussed everything."[5]

There is, of course, a spiritual crisis in the loss of voice. When we silence or censor the inner voice, we easily disconnect from the "still, small voice" within that is God. Spiritually, then, we are lost. If we do not know and affirm ourselves, we definitely will have trouble knowing God and believing that we are created in God's image. If we cannot listen to our own inner wisdom, we will not likely be listening to God's wisdom within us. Clement of Alexandria once said, "It is the greatest of all disciplines to know oneself. It is in knowing oneself that we know God." A wise teacher said that "our greatest temptation is *not* to be who we are called to be—our unique selves, with the image of God within us."[6] It is easy to see how women succumb to that transgression.

Fortunately, however, this trend toward loss of relationships, loss of self, and loss of connectedness to God is beginning to turn around. Carol Gilligan, Mary Belenky, the American Association of University Women, and many others who are researching and attending to these issues are inspiring us to reclaim our voices, to use our voices to tell about our lives and our feelings, and to be direct and courageous in speaking our truths to ourselves and to others. Also, Maria Harris, in her exploration of the impact of midlife and loss of voice, is assisting our spirits to move beyond silence and to claim a jubilant time of knowing both ourselves and our God as we move into our fifties and beyond.

(Susan) The beauty of quilts is evidence of the beauty within the quilt makers. Women and girls are incredible human beings, created by the same Holy One who makes glorious rainbows and thundering waterfalls and wonderfully intricate environmental systems. Not all that we shelter within us feels attractive or empowering. However, even when we experience the most loss, the deepest hurt, the most rage, or incredible sorrow, our "inner work" invariably is expressed in our art—and it is important work, ultimately holding its own beauty. We have listened to many quilters share their quilts and explain the joys, or struggles, or fears, or grieving that infused their artistic energy as they were creating their quilts. The "soul work" of quilting propels us to self-reflection, to listening to what our hearts and our words are revealing. In the silence of the sewing room or in the conversations around a quilting frame or classroom table, we often discover that what bubbles up from our souls is worth attending to, is worth giving voice to, is reflective of our deepest selves, and is integral to the beauty of our whole selves, our holy selves.

Quilt artist Erika Carter has reflected on her internal process of giving voice and validity to her creativity. Despite being adept at making tailored clothing and being an accomplished knitter, she never believed herself to be creative. Then she was led to her first quilt class and "recognized the call to work creatively within the quilt medium. So, the hard work began. Just as an artist in any medium must work diligently to find his or her voice, I knew I must make many quilts to understand what I wanted to say and how I wanted to say it."[7]

Quilt and fabric artist, as well as clergywoman, Laurie Bushbaum wrote, "Whatever else art may be, it is primarily the work of the soul. For me, art has been the way to find Soul, nurture it, heal it, grow it. To give it shape and color, texture and voice."[8]

When he was interviewing Alice Walker for his book, Roland Freeman asked her to comment on a feeling that he had experienced as a child, an "attraction to the environment women created in quilting." Walker responded:

What attracted you was the feeling that they [the women] generated. You were attracted to their eternity. They had taken back their eternity from the men around them. And this was the form that they used to have their eternity. . . . And when you get one of their quilts, you can see that this is what their eternity, externalized and made into a form, looks like, but in fact, they experienced their eternity long before you saw their quilt.[9]

What are women and men today creating in their quilts? Many voice their grief, their need for healing, their rage, their joy, their eternity, their need to provide warmth and healing for others. The list of voiced messages quilted into art could go on and on. Many, having found the power of their message in the process of quilting, go on to lift that voice and live out that empowerment in multiple avenues of their lives, around the quilt frame and beyond.

*"Passion," from the Emotion Series: A Visual Journal by
Suzanne Evenson, photographed by Chas Krider. Designed and
pieced to give voice to a passion for new life.*

THREADS OF REFLECTION

Centering Prayer

May your voice, O God, empower my own.

Scripture

Their voice goes out through all the earth, and their words to the end of the world.
—Psalm 19:4

Quilt Reflections

Enjoy and ponder the quilt entitled "Passion" on page 24.

The quilt artist Suzanne Evenson wrote this about the quilt, which is the seventh quilt in a series expressive of her life immediately before and following a divorce: "A decision to begin graduate school in Fine Art ignited creative fires in me that had previously been dormant. A passion for my new life and a new relationship is amply displayed by the choice of color now returned to my world."

What does this quilt say to you about your own voice?

When in your life have you felt voiceless or silent when you wanted to speak? Write about that time in your journal. What might a quilt look like that would express voicelessness?

When in your life have you spoken your truth or told your story, even when it was scary to do so? Write about that time in your journal. What might a quilt look like that would express your empowered voice?

Prayer

God of All Speech,

Guide me in the use of my own voice, in the reclaiming of my story. Give me courage when I might speak. Give me patience and gentleness with myself in my silences. May your love and the love of others inspire my expression of my true self. Amen.

CREATIVITY

See, I am making all things new.

—Revelation 21:5

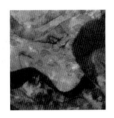

THREADS OF TRADITION

Quilters have cultural and family traditions and stories from which to draw inspiration for their new creations in cloth. Now at the beginning of the twenty-first century we can adapt these traditions and apply our own creative expressions to them in contemporary and individualized ways. We live in an age that encourages creativity as a way to expand knowledge about ourselves and to express our knowing about the world. Quilt makers have a unique opportunity to stretch out beyond known traditional approaches, thus creating yet new traditions that expand the horizons for future quilters.

Quintessential Quilters Guild in Columbus, Ohio, recently challenged its members to create a quilt called "Tradition with a Twist." The challenge was to take a traditional pattern and create a new design with it using three different designated fabric packets. The resulting quilts were highly varied and creative. Guild member Wendy Bynner designed the quilt "Quilt Til You Wilt." Recently retired from her career as a veterinary radiologist, Wendy found this process very liberating and fun as she went outside the boundaries of traditional expectations, exploring free-form quilting that she had never done before. Her completed quilt incorporated three-dimensional blocks, many symbols, and a nontraditional approach of appliquéing onto pieced blocks. Despite using required purple fabric that she did not like, Wendy was able to express her love for sewing and quilting in an original quilted piece.

THREADS OF OUR SOULS

In the same spirit, we found other quilt artists who share Wendy's willingness to engage in making all things new: "An artist isn't a special kind of person, each person is a special kind of artist."[1]

In gathering resources for our book, we discovered many special kinds of artists. Vikki Pignatelli and Father Larry Nolan remind us that our commitment to meet God in our creative pursuits can result in beautiful and aesthetic new forms of expression.

Father Larry's small hermitage on the grounds of St. Raphael retirement community in Columbus, Ohio, is a study in total devotion to his creative connections with God. Every room is filled with explorations into some form of art: photography, welded metal sculptures, hand-blown glass works, and most recently, quilted wall pieces. His cottage is not grand, but the rooms are packed with the raw materials of his crafts. About this devotion, he states, "My love of art comes from my earliest contact with the Bible, which says that God made it all with great love and care . . . everything has divine beauty to it. The artist at work is immersed in the experience of this divine wonder and beauty. . . . It is a very spiritual, uplifting thing."

This holy man arises before the sun each day to welcome the day's turning from darkness to light. In his hermitage he reads scripture and maintains a contemplative attitude, welcoming God into all of his activities throughout the day. He is exuberant about the way that God speaks to him through his journey into creative adventures. Unconcerned about such things in the artistic world as juried shows or artistic parameters that might in some way "rate" his creativity, Father Larry is a pure artist. He truly follows the Spirit in his process. He manifests what he feels God calls him to make in material form: "Creativity is where God meets me." The experience of hearing Father Larry's excitement about his creativity is reminiscent of Susan Gordon Lydon's observation: "There is an ecstasy in the act of creation that matches the intensity of religious rapture; both partake of divinity and are gifts granted by the Great Creative Spirit."[2]

Father Larry became intrigued with quilting while he was serving as photographer at the annual gathering of art quilters at Quilt Surface Design Symposium. Art quilters from around the world convene each spring in Ohio for this symposium, originated by art quilters Nancy Crow and Linda Fowler. They are immersed in many workshops discovering limitless ways of fashioning art with cloth surfaces. Father Larry was intrigued by the excitement he witnessed in the classrooms while these artists stitched and cut and explored the raptures of cloth in motion. He developed a friendship with the quilters, and they then became his teachers. His mandala (or circle) quilt, "In God's Eyes," on page 100 depicts how Father Larry imagines that God perceives the world: "All of it is sacred." "God saw it was good." All beings are encircled in God's compassionate eyes.

Vikki Pignatelli's story about creativity is also one of devotion to God. Vikki's quilt art pieces are pictorial representations of major life passages as well as the interior journey of her spiritual development. Formerly a painter, Vikki is a self-taught quilter who is now writing a book about the process she created of working with curved, flowing lines in her quilt art. She has shown her quilts in numerous international quilt events and is an award-winning artist.

Vikki believes that her call is to share her awareness of the presence of the Holy Spirit in her life through her quilts. However, as she began quilting, she was frustrated by being unable to find a traditional pattern that would adequately depict the brilliant undulating flames of Spirit and passion she was feeling in her soul. To convey the messages from this deep spiritual knowing, she needed to use a number of curved shapes, some three-dimensional, in brilliant primary colors. She created a design and a process of her own. Trusting her creative resources, this quilt artist was able to comply with her soul's urge for expression.

Vikki shares how she allows herself to be open to messages from the greatest Creator:

Each one of us glows with the spirit of creativity . . . very special gifts and talents given to us individually by our Creator. In my quilt, "The Fire Within," I depict this concept of creativity burning deep within us with a spiral. Our gifts and talents are the flames that radiate from our inner soul outward through the world, affecting others in ways we are not aware of. The spiral and many of the flames are dimensional, as we are dimensional, and rise off the quilt to show that our ability to touch others is boundless.

The "Fire Within" is dedicated to the Holy Spirit . . . the Spirit of my creativity. This quilt was technically easy to make. But emotionally, it was difficult for me. As I created "Fire Within" I sensed I was not alone, but indeed was working with a Co-Creator. I felt I was being guided in my artistic choices. I would become overwhelmed, awed and a little frightened as I watched our quilt unfold and take shape. Often, I'd break down in tears . . . tears were the only way my body could release the powerful flood of emotions and sense of wonder coursing through my mind and heart. I had to leave the house, and took many long walks to regain my composure and calm myself.

When we visited Vikki in her home, we realized that there is definitely sanctity about the space in which she does her creative work. Vikki shared her reverence for her work in hushed tones, tinged with awe. The room in which she works felt like sacred space to us. Her sewing/quilting room felt like a serene cloister.

I (Barbara) find this experience in my quilting space as well. Sitting before a stash of fresh fabric can be intimidating to me. When I forget that God is the Creator working through me, I am stopped cold, fearful of outcomes and stuck in my performance anxiety. However, when I invite God to join me in this space, there is the "remembering" that this is God's work, not mine. Knowing that I am merely the channel of God's expressive urges, I feel the "flow" return, and the fun begins. My sewing space is graced with a new light and freedom to move out into the unknown. Creativity calls for self-forgetting and deeper self-remembering. (I am always thankful that God tolerates a pretty messy room in which the creativity happens!)

Creativity includes an attitude of reverence that we bring with us to the process. Wonderful new possibilities arise when we see our whole world (or even one room or a corner of one room) as a sacred space. When we invite God into our daily activities as we suspend our ordinary perceptions, we lay the groundwork for surprise and novelty and new ways of experiencing something beyond the everyday self.

Creativity is also about refusing to be called away by the mundane, the chores that too often remove us from our God-centered expressive selves. Pamela Hardiman believes that "quilting is fundamental to my life and creative expression. I'm willing to tolerate a pretty dirty floor to be able to quilt. The floor will wait." The creative urge longs for a response. Pamela goes on to explore how this process is for her: "Creation is the work of God, and as human beings made in God's image, we are capable of creating on a human plane. I believe that whenever we are using our gifts and stretching ourselves creatively, we are engaged in a spiritual pursuit. . . . When I was a child, I posed the question to myself, 'What is my favorite part of my body?' My answer, then and now, is my hands. It is my hands that allow me to make quilts and express myself in a potent visual way."

There is a generosity of God, our creative source, when we allow ourselves to forget time limitations and steep ourselves in the wonder of new ways of seeing, when we allow our hands to be used as God's instruments of creative expression. This open place where God meets us is a very broad intersection, one with unlimited access and multiple paths—none of them wrong ways to go. There is a freedom in losing ourselves in these new explorations, knowing that each one of us is a unique expression of God.

"When we are in the creative process . . . we sit at the intersection of heaven and earth acknowledging our connection with all that is as we determine which way to turn to express a tiny piece of the Holy within all things."[3]

Creative adventures translate the ordinary experience into something holy. Sue Bender talks about sacramental acts. "Sacrament" as defined in the dictionary is "a practice that is considered especially sacred as a sign or symbol of a deeper reality." Bender maintains that "everyday activities and objects take on sacred significance and are thus entitled to reverence when we approach them with mindfulness and intentionality."[4]

Indeed, as we explore the nature of quilting, we find that women's spirituality in particular seems to recognize the sacredness of everyday life. Homemakers the world over redefine objects in their environment, reshaping scraps and remnants of fabric into new forms of warm clothing and bedding for their families and loved ones. These recycling activities become sacraments as we stay aware of God at work in our lives and through our stitching and as we pray about the relationships that have such profound meaning in our lives.

Finally, let us remember that creativity is a juicy process. The image of a drippy, sweet Georgia peach, succulent and just-right ripe at the first bite, speaks to us of God's awesome creativity. As we first experience eating the peach, we are aware of many things: how this peach looks, smells, tastes; how it fills the belly. When we are in the experience of eating the peach, we come to recognize the infinite ways that the Creator God imaginatively seeks to feed our bodies and souls. And just as we give thanks for God's nurturing of our creative expression, we are called to respond with our own soul-filled imaginings.

*"The Fire Within" by Vikki Pignatelli. Designed and quilted
by Vikki, using her unique curved piecing technique. The artist
dedicates this quilt to the Holy Spirit.*

THREADS OF REFLECTION

Centering Prayer

God of all creation, I thank you for your juicy presence in my soul. May each object I encounter today remind me that you are creating without ceasing in the world and within me. Show me how to use my unique gifts in sacramental ways.

Scripture

For everything created by God is good, and nothing is to be rejected, provided it is received with thanksgiving; for it is sanctified by God's word and by prayer.

—1 Timothy 4:4–5

Reflection

Take a few moments to sit quietly with Vikki's quilt on page 32.

What feelings surface as you view it?

What do the colors and design suggest to you?

If you were to create a quilt or painting of some passion or "fire within" yourself, how would it look?

Prayer from Vikki Pignatelli: An Artist's Meditation

Heavenly Creator, open my eyes to the beauty around me. May I have a sense of your splendor and majesty as I ponder the mysteries of our world and the universe. Let me rejoice in the simple wonders you've created instead of dwelling on the unimportant. Allow me to recognize your presence in the everyday miracles that happen.

You have made me in your image and have blessed me with your special gift of creativity. Let your artistry influence my creative thoughts so that I may imitate you in my work and life. Help me use my unique gifts, talents and abilities in a way that reflects my love for you. Inspire me to be an instrument for your work here on earth.

IMAGES OF GOD

Then God said, "Let us make humankind
in our image, according to our likeness."

Genesis 1:26

THREADS OF TRADITION

For generations, women have delighted in quilt making as a channel for the creative process, an outlet for the God-given, artistic talents within. From the moment of inspiration ("Yes, I want to make *that* quilt!") through the delight and discovery of fabric selection ("I love those colors and prints!") to the discipline of countless hours spent cutting and sewing together hundreds of small pieces of cloth, creativity is unfolding. An art form that began as a necessity for our foremothers was soon transformed into an artistic outlet for creative expression.

From our past to the present, pioneer women, Amish women, African American women, Hawaiian women, Mennonite women, and many more women—and some men—of all walks of life in this country and beyond have relished the opportunity to stitch together colorful arrangements of cloth into a thing of service and beauty. Today, computers make variations on traditional patterns endless and the creation of new designs practically instantaneous. Quilting and fabric art have moved in exciting directions as quilters all over the world strive to "reclaim forms and symbols traditionally trivialized as sentimental or as merely feminine and decorative."[1]

Whether we design and arrange fabrics in our heads, on graph paper, or on a computer, whether we use traditional patterns and fabric or "push the boundaries of high art,"[2] what remains intact is the creative spirit of the quilter/artist. For many quilters, that creative spirit is an expression of God's Spirit. As we breathe life into quilts and designs, we are acting in the image of the Creator God.

THREADS OF OUR SOULS

Barb tells this story of birthing a quilt with her mother:

> One warm summer evening a few years ago, my mom, Lila, urged me to join her in the creation of a wall hanging that called for at least two hundred two-inch squares of many colors and prints. I was a very reluctant student. I could not imagine that I would have the patience or desire to create anything from this heap of mismatched tiny pieces of fabric. However, it is not easy to deter or distract my mother when she is ready to create. Thus, with her encouragement, we set out to design a "watercolor" quilt, in which the two-inch squares of light and dark fabric are

placed in such a way that a meaningful design is born. We strove to pro-
duce a light, white-gold center that gradually went to darker shades of
blues and purples as we moved closer to the four corners of the piece.
Before us were many squares of fabric—colorful pieces of cloth lovingly
given to her by her quilting friends.

The creation of the design was like a dance, moving a swatch here
or there, each of us putting one piece down, taking one piece up, silently
circling around the fresh, empty design area until we felt an image
emerging. At once, I became a part of this dance of creativity. I soon
came to realize that there was a lively internal process going on as we
wordlessly moved around the design table. Swirls of colors emanated
from the center of the design. We kept stepping back from the field to
sense the bigger pattern, sliding back to the edge of the table to move a
yellow here, a burgundy there.

We moved in silence, as though we were listening for the next
bar of music that would introduce the next step. All the while, the
sense of rhythm both soothed and inspired me as I watched this lovely
piece come to life. A few hours passed before either Mom or I came
back to the "real space" in which we were working. We stood apart
from the new creation before us. As we came out of this meditative
rhythm, we were pleased with the way the colors flowed and blended
into one another.

We celebrated the rhapsody that was part of the creative space.
Silent music, silent witness. Silence makes space for the process of creativity to birth itself in us. We start in the silent deep place of our

mother's womb. Quilts start in the silent core of our being and are birthed through our receptivity to the possibilities that reside in color and fabric and shapes. The Dancing Creator within is our divine seed. Inspiration, imagination, and connections arise from this fertile center, this deep, dark, juicy place that beckons us to dance with colors and flows with the watery washes before us.

Who is God? What is God like? Since the beginning of time, humankind has pondered these questions. Since the beginning of time, we have heard the oft-repeated responses: "God is like a Father," "God is like a Son," "Man is created in the image of God." For many women, being created in the image of God is unimaginable. How does a woman affirm all that is within her—the power to be, to create, to love, to heal, to nurture, to run and jump and climb great heights—when the ideal held up to her is of a man and a Man-God?

During the years of my (Susan's) late twenties, countless images of God became deeply painful to me, cutting me off more and more from any sense of the Holy. My polite pleas for language changes and inclusiveness turned to anger and frustration as the congregation I served and most of my colleagues turned deaf ears: "It's not our issue," "We can't offend others as we accommodate you," "You can't take people's Father God from them!" Imagining God in new and meaningful ways became my soul work. Such work was often solitary, going-into-my-depths work. Gradually, however, I discovered and joined other women on the same journey. Some men and many laywomen, clergywomen, and women theologians and biblical scholars have been doing re-imagining work for several decades.

Quilters, too, often believe that quilting is soul work. We go deep into ourselves, into silent places, sometimes into chaos and despair, to reach for the experiences of our lives that are reflected in our art. As we quilt, the time alone or the time with other quilters is sacred time, time when we frequently wrestle with the meanings of our experiences, touch our true feelings, discover the many facets of our responses to life events, offer our "sighs too deep for words" and our prayers of rejoicing. Many quilters believe that God is at work in these moments, in our reflections, sharings, creations.

Quilting has given me (Susan) experiences and images of the Holy that are both challenging and exciting. As I pondered Barb's reflections on quilting with her mom, on dancing around the design table and creating a kaleidoscope of color and fabric and meaning, a new image of God cascaded into my life. The image flows, as I imagine God flows, dances as I imagine God dances, and creates, blesses, and communes as I imagine God does—with each creative undertaking, each new baby born, each rebirth of spirit in the universe, each new universe in the cosmos.

One morning a few years ago Barb came upon a prayer that spoke of the woman who raises her arms in prayer and brings light to the world. While she pondered this image, she looked down at her feet, where a current issue of *Noetic Sciences Review* had fallen open to a wonderful painting of a woman sitting cross-legged on a platform. The earthy woman faces east with her arms uplifted as in prayer, holding two antlers. Barb felt compelled to capture this "Aha!" moment of connection in a quilt seen on page 40. "Our Muse" immediately became an important presence on our writing team, hanging in Barb's sewing/writing room. She depicts the Holy, inspiring our prayers, our dancing, and imaginings as the book came to life.[3]

God is like a quilter designing a new creation. God is like a woman, a muse, a mother, who dances and floats around a table of color and fabric until the creation is the perfect reflection of the hope, of the dream held in her heart and in her imagination.

Imagining is the stuff of life and the life force of quilters and artists. In our imaginations, our best hopes and dreams and designs become linked with life, with those whom we love and value. Our gifts of creativity and artistry—gifts we all possess in one form or another—find their source in the Divine, reflecting the image of the Holy in each of us. Quilters know the power of re-creation, know the incarnation of the Holy as fabric and color and design come together into a new creation. It is a power beyond ourselves, yet within us. It is a reflection of our best selves and a reflection of the Divine Other as well.

The image of God in each of us comes alive for me (Susan) around a quilting frame or in a quilting class around a table. As I watch each woman's face take on the light of creative energy, the joy of shared passion, the reality of truths about life shared and held sacred, I know God. I see God. It is the same Goddess that I see shining back at me in the eyes of my daughters. She is a magnificent cocreator, woman God, and I am delighted to be "in her image."

"Our Muse" by Barbara Davis. Machine pieced, appliquéd, and quilted.
Based on the acrylic painting Antler Woman *by Lee Lawson.*

THREADS OF REFLECTION

Centering Prayer

As you inhale, pray, "In your image . . ." As you exhale, pray, "I am created."

Scripture

In the image of God . . . male and female God created them.
—Genesis 1:27

Quilt Reflections

Ponder and enjoy Barb's quilt on page 40.

How is the woman depicted like or different from your images of God?

Imagine God as a quilter, as a grandmother, as a gardener, as a sister. What images well up from your own experiences of what is sacred to you?

What does it feel like to try on a new image of God?

Prayer

Dancing, Creating God,

Stir your creative energy within me. Aware of being "in your image," I delight in all of the ways that I reflect you to the world, in all of the ways that I experience your presence in my daily life. Bless the women who have been affirming models of what is holy and sacred in all of your creation. Amen.

· MYSTERY ·

*Think of us in this way, as servants of Christ
and stewards of God's mystery.*

I Corinthians 4:1

THREADS OF TRADITION

Mystery quilting is one technique that challenges us to abide not knowing what our "product" will look like until it is completed. With most other quilting techniques, the creator has at least some sense of and control over the composition and design and placement of the fabric pieces. In mystery quilting, however, it is necessary to inch forward block by block while relying solely on clues distributed by the teacher who has already seen the completed pattern. This technique requires trust in that one individual who knows the outcome. The instructor must offer enough guidance and support in the selection of color tones and patterns to lead the quilter to appropriate fabrics of lights and darks that will "work" for the pattern. This technique is about surrender, trusting the process, and giving up control. Many quilters find it very revealing in ways that are instructive beyond just learning to create a quilted piece. Some find it too confining and others find it a challenge to abide the not knowing, to live in the surprise of what is yet to be seen. In any case, it challenges the quilter to be a good steward of mystery.

THREADS OF OUR SOULS

> A salt doll journeyed for thousands of miles over land, until finally it came to the sea.
>
> It was fascinated by this strange moving mass, quite unlike anything it had ever seen before. "Who are you?" asked the salt doll. The sea replied smilingly, "Come in and see." So the doll waded in. The farther it walked into the sea the more it dissolved, until there was only very little of it left. Before that last bit dissolved, the doll exclaimed in wonder, "Now I know what I am."[1]

We spend our entire lives wading through questions about our identity. There is a danger for women in our culture of our individual identities being dissolved and absorbed into the needs of others, because we are the "caretakers" of the world. We forget or reject the need to claim our own boundaries. Claiming and naming our boundaries is a most significant learning for many of us as women, and it requires no small amount of reconditioning of our own preconceived notions of roles. Once we become aware of being cherished as daughters of God, we then know we are valued for who we are, not what we do. We are then more open to the mystery of where God will take us next. Ultimately, we will all journey home again to God, to the ultimate Knowing of who we are in God.

We seek to uncover the mystery that envelops our existence. God continues to beckon us to dip our toes into the water and wade more deeply into this mystery of who we are. From the vantage point of middle age, however, it seems likely that it may only be in the final moments of life that we will have a revelaton of the mystery of who we "really are" in God's eyes.

By midlife, many people find that the spiritual journey involves periods of walking through an unlit tunnel without seeing its end, punctuated with wonderings about our purpose and life's ultimate meaning. We search for assurances of our worthiness and call. We look for signs that God is at work in our lives or that God is indeed *in* our lives and our struggles.

In a recent conversation, Barb's husband, Terry, said, "If you want to discover who you are, you must wrestle with mystery." We are confronted with the reality of mystery. What does it mean to accept mystery as an important aspect of life? How might we come to peace with the Not Knowing?

Quilting is one of the ways that we search, either consciously or unconsciously, for clues to our meaning. Through this work of hand and heart, we learn that we cannot predict or control how God is/will be at work in our lives, but we can get clues that deepen our understanding about how to move forward in the presence of uncertainty.

Carol Gura holds annual spiritual retreats in Cleveland, Ohio. Quilting is the central "connector" for the participants of these retreats. In a recent retreat, called "Pieces and Patterns of Our Lives,"[2] the mystery quilt concept was the vehicle for much spiritual reflection for the participants. New awarenesses came to life as the women "prayed their way" step by step. When the completed quilt tops were shared in a group, there were many revelations. Each quilt, though done with the same instructions, was unique because of the fabric choices the women had made and the placement of the colors. The quilt makers remarked on how being unable to control or predict the way that their final product would look was challenging. Their choices were limited, and yet they had entrusted their instructor with the wisdom to make it all come together in a positive way. Ursaline Sister Charlotte Trenkamp, or "Sister Stitch," said about this process: "The whole idea of letting go seems to be developing for each person in a different way." For Sister Stitch, "It's a good discipline, excellent for a take-charge person who is used to envisioning the final result and controlling the construction."[3]

Perhaps in our yearning to discover how God is at work in our lives, we might turn to such an approach as the mystery quilt. We proceed, often in the dark, making our way step by step, unable, in reality, to move forward any other way.

This Spirit-filled journey involves deep trust, but frequently, we become frightened, afraid that God may have forgotten to distribute the next clue. Thus, we attempt to circumvent this process, to anticipate the clues and hem in what we believe to be God's next step.

This circumvention is folly. We may imagine that we can predict outcomes or control the design or in some way command how life will unfold. As the mystery quilt process teaches us, it is only when we acknowledge our limitations and begin to rely on the Great Teacher that we can relax into God's veiled or mysterious process. It is paradoxically then that life will and does unfold in ways we often cannot possibly foresee.

Letting go and living in mystery has long been a challenge for me (Barb). If I give up control, will I relinquish what little management of my image that I have to offer? Will my inadequacies become more glaring when I can no longer hide behind the facade of "having it all together"? Immersed in quilt making, I find that the more I let go, the more the concern about having it all together fades into the background. I begin to accept that it is okay *not* to have it all together, knowing there is the possibility of having some of it together in small bits and pieces!

"Strips that Sizzle" by Barbara Davis. Machine pieced and quilted.
Based on a design of the same name by Margaret Miller,[4] this quilt is
reminiscent of a "God's Eye" weaving.

THREADS OF REFLECTION

Centering Prayer

I know you are there, God. Help me tolerate my not knowing everything else.

Scripture

Now I know only in part; then I will know fully, even as I have been fully known.

—1 Corinthians 13:12

Quilt Reflections

Reread the story of the salt doll. What do you hope to know about yourself? What do you *already* know about yourself and your relationships?

Sit with the "Strips that Sizzle" quilt on page 46. What does this quilt say to you about mystery or self-discovery? If you were to create a quilt about mystery, what colors, textures, and design would it have?

Write a short journal entry about being known by God.

Prayer

Mystery lives. I abide in this mystery, knowing that I am already known to you, God. This is a wondrous comfort to me. Walk with me in the anticipation of my discoveries of you and who I am. Be with me as I learn to abide not knowing everything.

COMMUNITY

A faith that lived first in your grandmother Lois.

2 Timothy 1:5

THREADS OF TRADITION

No image is more closely associated with the art of quilting than that of the quilting bee. It requires little effort to imagine a bee with lively friends gathered around a quilting frame, working on someone's quilt, meeting new neighbors, catching up on the news of each other's life, sharing stories of joy and sorrow, laughing together, crying together, remembering, relaxing in the comfort of each other's company. In the early days of America's history, and in the many other countries from which the tradition of quilting originated, quilting offered an opportunity for friendship and community that was eagerly anticipated. It was not unusual in North America's pioneer days for women to travel many miles to be a part of the cherished camaraderie around the quilting frame.

In the lives of African slaves in the South, quilts provided a sense of community and a means by which stories and traditions from Africa could be preserved. Permitted to quilt only on their own time (late at night or when all other assigned tasks were completed), slave women and men gathered for quilt parties whenever possible. The earlier

4 8

part of a quilt party "was devoted to work on the quilt, the latter part to festivity and dancing."[1] Perhaps the most important function of those gatherings around quilting was the opportunity to preserve a sense of identity and to pass on African lore as well as "moral lessons, values, attitudes, strategies for survival, rites of passage, and humor!"[2] Community news was shared on such occasions, news of "births, deaths, illnesses, social events, and secret meetings. And most important, slaves in the quarters learned from house servants what was going on in the big house."[3]

In her book *Spirits of the Cloth,* author and quilt artist Carolyn Mazloomi refers to the bonding nature of quilting bees and to an essay written by Bernice Steinbaum. Steinbaum believes that quilting bees may have been "the first feminist consciousness raising group."[4] "For slave women in particular," Mazloomi continues, "they were festive occasions that allowed them to escape from fieldwork and achieve a sense of community."[5] Life was sustained, friendships were built, and spirits were consoled as needle and thread took to cloth.

THREADS OF OUR SOULS

Humankind is created for community, for living in relationship with God, with self, and with others. Our souls are nurtured and challenged and healed when we surround ourselves with friends, loved ones, and other people of faith. Additionally, in our fast-paced world where there is precious little time for reflection and self-care, many of us who are introverts crave solitude, yearn for a time apart from worldly distractions and demands. Even extroverts, who get energy from ideas and others outside themselves, need the balance of some solitude in their lives. It takes a certain discipline and intentionality to ensure that space for both communal time and solitude is created with some regularity in our lives.

As hard as it is to create that needed solitude, authentic, faith-filled community seems equally elusive. European American culture, with its emphasis on individualism and self-sufficiency, deters the creation of sustained, nurturing communal life and relationships.

Spiritual formation—our continual striving to conform to or be formed in the image of our Creator—sets us on a journey. The journey entails numerous choices that define and refine our values; countless challenges to our belief system; endless situations that pose faith questions, provide spiritual inspirations, and surface our commitments, passions, and identities. Sometimes those experiences result in patterns of life that stand against the status quo. To be sustained on that journey, we need each other. We need the wisdom and perspective and faithfulness of friends and family and those outside ourselves. Others in trusted community can offer us both the inspiration and the challenge needed to refine our values, beliefs, and interpretations of life, ever saving us from the misguided notion that we have "arrived."

Faith communities, where one might expect to encounter transforming, sustaining, and challenging experiences of spiritual friendship, also are affected by our culture's radical notion of independence and self-sufficiency. At most religious gatherings, we repeatedly tell each other that we are "fine, thanks," no matter how brokenhearted we may be. Trust-filled, deep sharing of one's spiritual journey is not possible within a cordial, brief "coffee hour" relationship. Even in the adult education class or a meeting of the deacons of the church, the trust level is such that we seldom provide the give-and-take necessary for deep spiritual nurture or for the challenging exchange and accountability necessary for true Christian community. Often spiritual nurture is assumed or assigned to happen during the worship hour.

Many quilters, on the other hand, know quite well the value of interdependence and community. The leader of a spiritual quilting retreat, Carol Gura, is convinced that "women connect on a very deep level right away" when they gather to quilt. The retreat format for quilting and spirituality is a natural one, she believes, because quilting "has been continually perceived as a communal effort, which is very different from making a sweater by yourself"[6] or other more solitary art forms. An attendee of the retreat, Kathy Richmond, said that from the retreat "the biggest thing I get is camaraderie," which she describes as friendships that deepen and grow through the years.

In the tradition of a friendship quilt, which is created with blocks bearing the signatures of friends and family who have worked on the quilt, Richmond originated the concept of a healing quilt for the group. She designed a quilt using the Ohio Star pattern (the retreat happens in Cleveland), and each retreatant signed a star and then sewed it together. Around the border of the quilt was stitched the serenity prayer, and since then the quilt is sent to "whoever needs it that month, to be surrounded by the spirituality and support of the group."[7]

Quilters are known for creating quilts that extend their community to include the homeless, the poor, the infant at risk, the refugee, and others at the edges of society. Also, the community of quilting extends both backward and forward in time, crossing generations past, present, and future. Many quilters, while working on a quilt, remember those before them who were their quilting teachers or family members who shared a passion for quilting. Stories abound about sitting at the feet of a mother or grandmother, other relative or friend, as the art was learned and the sense of community was experienced. With the longevity of quilts, it is common to hear about the memories of a loved one from decades past whose very presence is felt as one is wrapped in the quilt created by her hands. Quilter Roberta Gerhardt wrote to us about completing a quilt begun by her son's next-door neighbor, Ruth. After Ruth's death, at the request of Ruth's family, Bobbi reluctantly undertook the completion of the neighbor's last quilt. To her surprise, as she worked on Ruth's quilt, a sense of "overwhelming closeness" developed for this unknown woman. Bobbi returned the quilt to the family with "much love" and many prayers when it was completed.

After returning from a trip to Russia, friend and church executive Tom Dipko had many stories to tell. One that stands out involved a Russian church member responding to a question from the North American group about why there are so many icons in the Russian Orthodox Church. The response was, "They are like family to us. We would no more think of worshiping without first greeting the saints than you would think of entering a room of your relatives without greeting each of them." The faith community includes the community of the saints. Often our spirits are

"Fiftieth Anniversary Quilt." Designed and quilted by Peggy Notestine, with blocks contributed by friends and extended family members on the occasion of her parents' fiftieth wedding anniversary.

quickened and nurtured by a sense of the surrounding presence of those who have lived and loved and believed in previous generations.

The line of continuity, so important in faith traditions, is mirrored in the experience of quilters who often know without a doubt the nearness of quilters who have gone before us.

THREADS OF REFLECTION

Centering Prayer

As you inhale, pray, "God of my ancestors . . ." As you exhale, pray, "Be present with me."

Scripture

I am reminded of your sincere faith, a faith that lived first in your grandmother Lois and your mother Eunice and now, I am sure, lives in you.
—2 Timothy 1:5

Quilt Reflections

Ponder the signatures and the tree of life in the center of the quilt on page 52.

This quilt was created by Peggy Notestine and her sisters for their parents' fiftieth wedding anniversary. Both family and friends offered messages of love by signing this beautiful friendship-style quilt.

What experiences of friendship and/or family mean the most to you?

What experiences of community are a part of your life journey?

Write about those experiences in your journal.

What might a quilt look like that would express your sense of community?

Prayer

God of all time and space,

Thank you for the moments of community, however fleeting or continuous, that grace my life. For those in my circle of family and friends who nurture, challenge, and inspire me, I give you thanks. Amen.

HEALING

To another gifts of healing by the one Spirit.

1 Corinthians 12:9

THREADS OF TRADITION

Watercolor quilting is a fairly new technique that has grown in popularity over the past fifteen years and is credited to quilters Donna Slusser and Pat Magaret.[1] This technique produces completed compositions that look like watercolor paintings. Done entirely with two-inch squares of many colors, prints, and patterns blended together to form a landscape of nature, portraiture, or abstractions, this technique is literally a work of bits and pieces. The overall impact is similar to that of an impressionist painting. Somewhat like viewing a Monet painting of water lilies, viewing impressionist quilts leads one to a sense of peace and visual harmony.

The artist often creates a drawing of the hoped for "painting" prior to beginning the actual quilt. A penciled grid of two-inch squares is overlaid onto this drawing. From hundreds of squares at hand, the quilter may choose the necessary number, then proceed to place the squares on another grid prior to sewing the squares together. The process requires a keen eye for the blending of color and pattern. Often a reversed magnifying glass is used to give distance to the completed piece. An alternative way to view the quilt is for the quilter to step far away from the work at hand. Either way lends a better perspective on how the squares complement one another.

THREADS OF OUR SOULS

"Our lives become rich and meaningful when we piece together the joys and sorrows, the questions and answers, the successes and failures, the longings, the people and experiences that have been the colors and shapes of our lives. Out of chaos we can sometimes make comforting patterns. Out of despair, beauty; out of longing, new possibility; out of joy, visual radiance."

—Rev. Laurie Bushbaum[2]

Watercolor quilting as a technique offers many metaphors for how we strive to be whole; how we piece together our joys and sorrows into meaning. To see our personal illnesses or emotional crises in a new way may involve stepping back, as is done when creating a watercolor quilt. We need to look from a new, more distant perspective at our lives to perceive what this life challenge might mean to us. Gaining insight may well be enhanced by wise counsel from others. Allowing family, friends, and community to "turn our experience over," as in a reversed magnifying glass, provides a deeper, more objective way to see how patterns in our lives blend or clash with one another.

In watercolor quilting, all squares are of equal importance. If one square is missing, the entire landscape is altered. This is also true in our search for integrity (or wholeness of body and mind) in our lives. We do not live in a vacuum, emotionally, physically, or spiritually. As quantum physicists are now espousing, every cell is affected by the action of all other cells, and each cell is essential to the integrity of the whole organism.[3] As "organisms," we human beings are all interconnected with one another. Thus, our well-being is in part defined by our interaction with others. Whether or not we are aware of it, we are definitely impacted by all that happens within and around us.

We are surrounded by community, seen and unseen, known and unknown, that influences our energies and abilities to regain balance. The ways in which we interface with our family, our faith community, our work world, and our environment will have an impact upon our health and healing. These relationships will determine our degree of balance or dis-ease.

We know in our own lives that a serious physical illness or emotional crisis in the family will definitely, albeit sometimes very subtly, impact each member's perception of the immediate world and, ultimately, perceptions about God. Wholeness is derived from a sense of identity and belonging within the family and the community at large. Each square or person has intrinsic value and importance to the health of the whole organism. Isolation breeds imbalance, and loneliness produces dis-ease, distress, or nonwholeness.

The following stories illustrate how wholeness and a sense of physical integrity were regained through God's gifts of community and quilting. A note: physical health is not always the "answer" that comes from God. Sometimes healing happens, not physically, but spiritually and emotionally when we recognize God is still in the inevitable process of our aging or declining health.

A Watercolor Message

Jinny Smanik loves to do watercolor quilting. She was diagnosed with cancer in 1995, and she had surgery to remove the tumor that year. Her quilting and the message that she received as she stepped back from her completed quilt became a crucial part of her recovery. Her faith and her connection with her family, friends, and quilting community were distinct ingredients in her recovery process. She reached out to others who also were quilters—to a network of people, most of them unknown to her except as Internet pals. Yet she received tangible prayers from these new companions in the shape of two-inch squares of cloth from around the country.

> Quilting was a big part of my healing after my cancer. I actually put [with the help of friends] a watercolor grid in the room I was recovering in, and began a watercolor quilt that chronicled my experience. Many of my "on-line" watercolor [squares] swap friends have had cancer and shared their experiences. They also sent me cards and two-inch squares when I had my surgery.
>
> I didn't plan the quilt design at all, just looked at the colors of the flowers friends had sent, thought through my feelings and began. The quilt is freeform, and actually just completed. I added stippling for top quilting in variegated bright metallic thread.
>
> I began with fabrics that said "cancer" to me, then ones that depicted the bright process of healing [with support from loving friends], and then into peaceful clouds to finish. When I had completed

the sewing of the quilt I tacked it to the wall to look at it, and saw a cross right in the middle of the dark red cancer portion. This was clearly God working through me and sending me a message about God's presence in my life even then. It was truly a life-transforming experience.

The Love Quilt

Elizabeth Allen suffered through a major illness. She was overwhelmed by the love and comfort she received from friends in her hometown, many of whom she had not seen since childhood, thirty years prior to her illness.

At last I had reached my goal, being able to dress myself, and the doctors allowed me to return home. I had had a thymoma tumor removed from my chest. This tumor which had made me allergic to myself, and kept my muscles from allowing me to walk, talk or eat normally was labeled benign and I was expected to return to full recovery. However, one complication followed another with serious infections, three more operations and significant time in intensive care. I finally returned home after five months in the hospital.

Shortly after [I arrived at home] a surprise package arrived from my hometown in Grand Island, New York. I pulled out the most gorgeous, colorful log cabin–patterned quilt. The back of it was covered with over seventy get well messages and signatures from my childhood friends whom I had not seen in years. A letter enclosed conveyed that an article had been written in the hometown newspaper about my illness along with an invitation to anyone who wished could come to one quilter home to send wishes and greetings by signing the quilt for me. "The

Love Quilt, according to Kathy its creator, was a way that the whole community could unite to share their prayers and greetings."

Two months following the arrival of the love quilt, Eliz wrote, "I know it brought healing powers with it. Just last week I went back to my doctor for another check-up. He exclaimed over and over that I was a 'Miracle.' He was astounded at the return of my strength in such a short time. I have followed his instructions, but I believe the Love Quilt brought a healing power that wasn't found on Dr. Mendel's prescription pad."

*"My Healing Quilt." Designed, pieced, and machine quilted
by Jinny Smanik. During recovery from surgery for cancer, Jinny used
two-inch squares from quilters across the country to create this piece.*

THREADS OF REFLECTION

Centering Prayer

I soften my eyes and look out into the distance. I welcome a new view of the world. I feel the connection with all that is within and around me.

Scripture

I set before you life and death, blessings and curses. Choose life.
—Deuteronomy 30:19

Quilt Reflection

"Out of chaos we can sometimes make comforting patterns. Out of despair, beauty; out of longing, new possibility; out of joy, visual radiance," comments Rev. Laurie Bushbaum.

Sit with Jinny's watercolor quilt on page 60. Look with soft eyes at her work. Are you able to discern the cross in the quilt that she saw and described in her own story? How do you feel as you search for a specific clue in the quilt? Or in your life right now?

Think of a time in your life that you have found a comforting pattern out of the chaos.

What did this pattern look like, or how did it feel or sound to you?

Write about those times. These are healing moments.

Prayer

Mysterious Healer,

We find you in the healing of our bodies and the calming of our spirits. May we be ever mindful of our part in the healing process. Remind us that we have the gifts of community, touch, words of support, and love to share to bring healing to one another and to the world. Amen.

FORGIVENESS

How often should I forgive?

Matthew 18:21

THREADS OF TRADITION

Quilts are often used in unexpected, nontraditional ways. Long appreciated for their warmth-giving qualities, quilts also have the potential to restore the soul. When a painful memory or experience is "wrapped" in a quilt, a gentle strength begins to warm the spirit. With that strength, some find the courage to begin the journey toward forgiveness and healing.

In his book *A Communion of the Spirits,* quilter Ronald Freeman shares a story connected to Hystercine Rankin's quilt, "Memories of My Father's Death." The quilt itself is powerful, depicting in fabric and words the story of her father's murder in 1939 at the hands of a white man. Freeman writes about visiting with Mrs.

Rankin and her husband one day and telling them of the impact her quilt was having in an exhibit. In talking with the Rankins, he asks them to take him to the place in the road where her father was shot. With some hesitation, Mrs. Rankin agrees. As they near the spot on "old Highway 20," they pass the house of the man who killed her father, a man who was never arrested or prosecuted. The two-story house appears recently landscaped and has a pond.

Mrs. Rankin whispers, "That's where that man lived who shot my father down. They done fixed it up and added on to it, but they can't hide the ugly facts."[1]

They travel down a hill and come to the spot in the road where her father had lain dying. It was Mrs. Rankin's first visit to the site since her childhood. Freeman writes,

> We laid the quilt top I'd just gotten from Mrs. Brinner on the road, as though we had covered the spot where her father once lay, and Mr. and Mrs. Rankin just stood there in silence for about ten minutes. Later I asked what she had been thinking as she stood on the road. "Looking down at that quilt, I was wondering how long after they shot him did my daddy live before he took his last breath. Maybe he could have been saved. That's what I was thinking."[2]

After riding back to the Rankins' home, mostly in silence, Mrs. Rankin gave Freeman a hug and thanked him for "helping her overcome a haunting nightmare."[3]

THREADS OF OUR SOULS

Forgiveness is a process, sometimes a very long process. It is not something one wills to happen; rather, it comes more as a gift, a grace.

Working on a quilt feels like being in constant prayer. When I (Susan) worked on a quilt for my husband, I thought and prayed a lot about our relationship, about what I was thinking and feeling, about the long years of his Ph.D. studies. Would we emerge from that process with a stronger marriage? Would we be able to forgive and move on from the stress and strain of those years? Would our daughters be able to name and deal with their own anxieties from a process that left both parents preoccupied with too much to do?

Quilting is such a slowing down process. It gives me time to focus. Somehow, exercising the creative side of myself, giving my artistic side expression, is empowering and comforting at the same time. I think about women over the centuries who have brought much to forgive and be forgiven to the quilt frame—hurts endured, unrelenting oppression, anger at God for a loved one's death. Did they quilt anger and frustration into their quilts? Did the process—over the weeks and months and years of piecing and quilting—lead to moments of forgiveness? When I have time with intimate friends around that quilt frame, when sharing deeply helps work things out, when quietness and comfort seep into life, am I more open to forgiveness or to being forgiving? Or when I quilt alone and each stitch is a prayer, am I in a more receptive position for God's spirit of forgiveness? I believe so.

The sacredness of life sometimes floods my soul as I quilt. Time on earth seems holy and fleeting, too short for hardness of heart and numbness of spirit. Forgiveness is not always a result of glimpses into the Sacred, but each glimpse opens me a little more, brings me closer to the One who has already forgiven me, helps me name and look honestly at different facets of my hurt or pain.

Some things that people do, or have done, are not humanly forgivable: the rape of a child, the abuse of a spouse, the denigration of one race or culture by another, the murder of a black man by a white man—the list could go on. In such instances, I wonder if even God's grace runs out. In such instances, often only God can forgive. And if forgiveness or peace or escape from a nightmare comes to a survivor, as to Mrs. Rankin, surely it is a gift from God, a gift that breaks through pain and hurt in some miraculous way. Quilts are sometimes channels for the Divine, something to wrap around us, to lie on the ground, to spread before us or surround us with the feel of comfort, peace, and hope.

A number of years ago, I (Susan) was moved by the apology made by my denomination, the United Church of Christ, to the peoples of the Hawaiian Islands for our complicity in their oppression. I have wondered many times, before and after that apology, whether the American Indians and African Americans in this country will ever receive an apology from white European Americans for their oppression, for the atrocities perpetrated on their ancestors in the name of Western expansion or economic necessity. And if not, will racism or sexism, heterosexism or classism ever be healed in North America? Will European Americans ever truly be whole and healthy people without repenting and confessing and seeking forgiveness for our legacy of oppression? I wonder. I worry. I pray.

In my prayers, I have come to experience compassion and have realized that forgiveness and healing can enter my heart in sometimes gentle and unexpected ways. There is, after all, only one person's healing I can really work on—my own. There is, too, one person I have to forgive first—myself. Out of my experiences of self-forgiveness and healing grow the compassion to be forgiving of another and the courage to enter into the often long, sometimes painful, process of reconciliation. As I work on forgiving myself, I pray for wisdom as well. Wisdom is the gift that helps me to discern whether prayerful waiting or overdue action is required in any relationship where the hoped for outcome is healing and wholeness. Quilting gives me the time for this internal, soul-encompassing work.

*"Our Healing Quilt" by Susan Towner-Larsen. Designed and
pieced by Susan. The colors and design have comforting, healing effects
important to her family.*

THREADS OF REFLECTION

Centering Prayer

As you relax and settle into your space, notice your breathing. Take a few deep breaths. Feel their cleansing power. When you are ready, pray as you inhale, "Still my spirit, God," and as you exhale, "Heal my heart."

Scripture

Let anyone among you who is without sin be the first to throw a stone at her.
— John 8:7

Quilt Reflections

Susan's quilt on page 66 is her family's "Healing Quilt," used to wrap around some- one who needs comfort, forgiveness, or healing.

What feelings emerge as you study the colors and design of her quilt?

What are your memories that need healing or forgiveness?

Focus on one memory and the feelings connected to it. Write in your journal about that memory and those feelings, or imagine a quilt design depicting them. What might your quilt look like? What colors would you use? How might you feel making the quilt?

What friend or family member might lovingly listen to your feelings?

Prayer

Thank you, God, for memories of health and joy, friendship and love. May those memories give me the strength and courage to face more painful ones. Help me to be gentle with myself, to trust that healing and forgiving are happening even when they're not obvious. Bless my reflections, my journaling, my quilting—aids to my internal process of working toward forgiving myself and others. Thank you for the wondrous gift of forgiveness that you have extended to me already. Amen.

LIBERATION

God has sent me to bring good news to the oppressed,
to bind up the brokenhearted,
to proclaim liberty to the captives,
and release to the prisoners.

Isaiah 61:1

THREADS OF TRADITION

Textile art in various forms serves as voices for liberation in many cultures. Throughout history, quilts and fabric creations have served as message bearers. In *Hidden in Plain View: A Secret Story of Quilts and the Underground Railroad*, Jacqueline Tobin and Raymond G. Doubard conjecture that quilts were actually encoded maps for escaping slaves during the mid-1800s in the United States.

Hispanic cultures also utilize their crafts of woven cloth as the storytellers about their struggles. *Arpilleras* (or story cloths) of the Andes people in Peru depict their harsh life and their struggles to overcome those who would attempt to erase their culture.

The Hmong people of Southeast Asia do beautifully intricate quilt work and also stitch stories on broad cloth panels of war and devastation, of soldiers marching into their villages and destroying their homes.

THREADS OF OUR SOULS

Secret messages encoded in quilts in southern United States, prayers and petitions embroidered in clothing in Mexico, and woven backpacks created by Guatemalan refugees—these are some of the ways that people living in suppressed and marginalized corners of the world name and deal with oppression.

Mercedes and *La Mariposa*

The women were of the *colonia* (settlement), La Laguinilla near Cuernavaca, Mexico. We were seated around a sewing table reading the Bible in their newly completed day care and work center. I (Barb) listened to their stories of emancipation and creativity and self-discovery. Each time I hear these stories, I am overcome by the awareness of God's presence in the midst of struggle and poverty.

This visit in 1985 was my fourth over a period of six years to this small, impoverished community. I (Barb) went as a participant on a mission trip to their community led by our friends Howard and Betsy Friend sponsored by the Karitas Foundation of Philadelphia, Pennsylvania.

I was compelled to go back to this place to learn more about how they found God amidst daily struggles to survive and care for their families. The women of La Laguinilla have long been part of a very "macho" culture. Their husbands thwarted every suggestion that these women, their wives, might leave their homes to earn money or build community. The women were seen as chattel, as possessions, and were not permitted to leave their homes for any reason except to attend church-related functions or tend to family needs. However, a local priest assisted them in forming a Christian-based community to study the loving, liberating message of the Christian Scriptures. Through their study of liberation theology, they came to know that Christ was walking among them. Empowered by his radical message of love and justice, they began to discover their gifts. These women reclaimed hidden gifts and began to use what they knew—how to sew, embroider, and create colorful clothing and household items from their limited resources. They now call themselves *La Mariposa*, the Butterfly, their symbol of new life.

The spouses of these women were initially very threatened by this activity. However, they soon began to show up at the workshop. As they realized the monetary potential that existed in the sale of the goods, some of the husbands joined the cooperative and learned new skills. This has not been an easy transition in any way. There are still struggles to learn how to establish a successful business. There are also other deeply rooted cultural issues that have serious impact upon their dreams to be independent entrepreneurs. The men of La Laguinilla are still threatened by the lack of available work in the community, and unemployment compromises their self-esteem. Alcoholism and domestic violence are common problems. However, in small steps, there is renewed hope for this tiny barrio that survives in the underbelly of a huge and wealthy tourist community in central Mexico.

Mrs. Williams and the Quilt Code

An equally inspiring tale comes out of the stories of how some African Americans may have developed a sophisticated code of secret messages during the long, long period of forced servitude that they endured in this country. The Underground

Railroad of the mid-1800s was actually a system of escape routes by foot, over land, crossing mountains and through rivers. Some slaves were secreted in covered wagons and commercial seagoing vessels. The Railroad was connected by "safe houses," homes and buildings where African Americans escaping from slavery in the South could hide and rest on their journey north to freedom. Conductors were the guides who gave secret information to the travelers and guided them to freedom.

Hidden in Plain View offers new perspectives about how the African American slaves may have used their quilts as maps to freedom. Author Jacqueline Tobin became acquainted with an African American woman living in Charleston, South Carolina, as she sat in the Charleston Marketplace selling her quilts. A spellbinding storyteller, Ozelle McDaniel Williams shared with Mrs. Tobin many, many fascinating connections between quilting and the Underground Railroad.

Mrs. Williams described how her ancestors had devised a brilliant code of quilted references used in their escape from slavery on the plantations of the South. Her stories revealed how this code employed the use of quilts commonly designed and favored in southern "white" patterns, such as "Wagon Wheels" and "Monkey Wrench." These patterns were employed to give messages to slaves about when to gather, what they needed for the escape to the North, when to leave, and what to bring along to assist them in their escape from a life in bondage. The "Quilt Code" included symbols and signs that they had brought from Africa and their ancestral heritage transposed onto "traditional" European American patterns of quilting that would seem "normal" to any outsider who might be observing their activities in the South.

Producing the "messages" in this way reduced the possibility that the plantation owners would suspect them of any trickery. This intriguing book suggests that a Quilt Code arose organically out of a longing for freedom. Mrs. Williams's stories and the authors' research present a strong argument that from the moment the first

Africans were sent away on slave ships from their homeland, the Africans worked in community and used their skills to plan for their own liberation.[1]

Resistance to oppression began as early as the 1600s, when the first wave of slave trade got under way, and continued through the 1800s and the evolution of the Underground Railroad. This yearning for freedom persisted into the twentieth century as the civil rights movement carried its cries for freedom across the country. Throughout all of these struggles, African Americans have used their ingenuity and creative gifts to empower and guide themselves with an eye toward their birthright, freedom.

Another more recent story about liberation and quilting happened in the South in the mid-1960s.

Callie Young and the Freedom Quilting Bee[2]

Mrs. Young was familiar with bondage. She had grown up as the granddaughter of a former slave. She was born in the early part of the twentieth century and had eleven children of her own. She had been trained in the skill of quilting at an early age, and as an adult, she used her trade as a way of supporting her daughter in college. During the civil rights movement in the 1960s, Mrs. Young organized her church quilting group to march alongside Dr. Martin Luther King Jr. It must have been an exhilarating experience, but the aftermath was not good. The churchgoing women were tormented and persecuted by their white neighbors because of their participation in the march.

An Episcopalian priest, Father Walter, who was involved in the civil rights movement, came to investigate rumors of oppression of and cruelty toward the African Americans of Wilcox County. Serendipitously, he found wonderful quilts hanging out on clotheslines at these women's homes. He learned that the women received an average of five dollars for their quilts in local sales. Father Walter devised a plan with a New York businessman to auction their quilts in the Big Apple. He purchased each quilt for ten dollars. That was in December 1965, and by the spring of the next year, Father Walter had garnered an average of twenty-seven hundred dollars each at auction for forty-two quilts made by the women of Possum Bend, Wilcox County, Alabama.

The women then put most of this seed money into the founding of the Freedom Quilting Bee in Wilcox County. Since that time the quilts of this tiny town have found homes in the White House and were sold in many upscale department stores. The number of quilters swelled to 125 as the prices of the quilts also increased. Because of the demand for these quilts, the production has moved from the homes and into more standardized production, but the originals are "deemed priceless treasures."[3]

*"Out of Africa" by Wyrelene Mays. Designed and hand quilted
based on a Hoffman Quilt Challenge. One of a series about Africa,
inspired by Mrs. Mays's own heritage.*

THREADS OF REFLECTION

Centering Prayer

Breathing in, savor "Freedom." Breathing out, send forth "Justice."

Scripture

I act with steadfast love, justice, and righteousness in the earth, for in these things I delight, says God.
—Jeremiah 9:24

Quilt Reflections

Spend time with Wyrelene Mays's quilt "Out of Africa" on page 74.

Note the black center of this piece that is hand quilted in the shape of Africa.

Close your eyes and imagine a slave en route to freedom on a starless night in 1862, or picture a quilter in Wilcox County, Alabama, in 1962. What might be the images that keep their spirits high and their faith alive?

What do you imagine their struggles must be? Their joys?

What might you learn from their determination, strength, and courage?

Think of your own heritage. Do you know what your grandparents or great-grandparents experienced in daily life?

Can you imagine how their efforts might have an impact on your existence today?

Prayer

God of all people, of all time, liberate me from my own prejudices and fears. Free me from old stereotypes and close-mindedness. Save all persons from injustice and from actions that demean and strip away self-worth. May such actions never take away our assurance that we are all your precious children.

· CENTERING ·

For where your treasure is, there your heart will be also.

Matthew 6:21

THREADS OF TRADITION

Hawaiian quilts are not pieced. Their beautiful designs are created by first folding a large piece of cloth in eighths and then carefully cutting out the pattern. This process is done in the same manner that many of us make paper snowflakes. The cutout design is unfolded, still in one large piece, and laid on top of another piece of background fabric, to which the design is hand sewn. The resulting two-color design conveys symbolism representative of the sacred traditions and stories of the Hawaiian people.

Like all indigenous beliefs, the Hawaiians believed: Hawai'i is the center of Mother Earth; Hawai'i is the gateway to the spiritual world; Hawai'i is the source of all the love and compassion in the world. . . . Without a center, peace, love and hope was unattainable. When one's center was balanced, the life force and life energy was able to flow freely. . . . The center of the quilt documented the center of mother earth and the center of one's self or the quilter. One's strength lies within the love and compassion of one's center, deep set and most of all forgiving.[1]

Also, Hawaiians believed that "certain areas on each island had gateways between the physical and the spiritual worlds, and that people could travel between the two." Hawaiian quilters therefore "created open centers on some of their quilts. The opening represented the gateway to the spiritual world."[2]

Some Hawaiian quilt designs have solid centers that represent "the core of the family, the center of one's life. It is the source, strength and the roots of the family and individual. That is why when a quilt was made, the center was always completed first because it was the quilter's center, and focus point, and they believed that is where their life and energy force came from."[3]

THREADS OF OUR SOULS

Quilter Lou Jane Gatford wrote, "I created a queen-size quilt for each child by the time they were seven. These I reluctantly had quilted by an Amish woman for reasons of time and space. Then I switched to lap quilting. I needed the quilting part as a way of keeping in touch with myself and my spiritual journey."

Time and again, women and men who quilt return to their quilt projects for a sense of centering, a time of pulling in all the frazzled fragments of a day and reconnecting with oneself and with God. The rhythm and motion of hand quilting, with the up and down, in and out rocking of needle and thread, can be especially comforting. (Susan) Sometimes, when all else in life feels out of control or overwhelming, the connection to fabric and design, the familiar rocking motion of stitching, and the spiritual, intimate realization that my foremothers shared the same comfort reground and center my soul. When each stitch is a prayer, or even when each stitch is a release of stress or anger, the sense of the sacredness of life begins again to seep into my consciousness. I can quilt for a while in anger or with pent-up frustrations, but usually, calmness sets in and whatever I have been feeling and experiencing becomes a part of prayer and reflection. My quilting meditations then often become centered in daily experiences. When there are lapses of days or even weeks without quilting, I find myself becoming uncentered. My morning prayer times often begin to lapse as well, and I yearn more and more for a sense of the Holy. Quilting often has the mysterious sense of "coming home," which I have come to recognize as the return to God, to myself, to the matters of the world from a position of wholeness or centeredness.

Centering conveys a sense perhaps of "having it all together." Although on many days I wish that getting it all together were possible, most often I do not experience being centered in that way. Centering, I believe, is a matter of grace. I come to my quilting with a tangle of emotions and worries and motivations, and God receives me just that way. Period. I do not have to filter or order or prioritize or clean up my thoughts. I can just be, and I place whatever I am pondering or stewing upon on that quilting hoop, offering it to a Sister-God who receives all of me with utmost graciousness and love. When that sense of being loved for who I am sinks in, I feel renewed and re-centered.

Centering is more than a focus on myself, although that is often the starting place. Meditations over one's quilting hoop or frame reach both backward and forward, both inside oneself and beyond oneself. The spirits of my quilting foremothers reach into my consciousness, and my dreams and hopes for my own daughters and women yet unborn take shape in my soul. Praying may begin with my own fears and worries and trials, but as time passes, my center shifts somewhat, and my prayers overflow with the world's realities.

Ultimately, centering is not about centering on oneself; it is about centering on God. I may need to begin with examining my soul, naming and releasing for a time what is foremost on my heart and mind, opening up to the needs and concerns of others beyond myself. Finally, however, rest in God, focusing on a sense of the Holy Other. Where those centered moments may take me is the work of the Spirit; how I get to those moments is frequently the work of needle and thread through fabric.

"Journey to the Center," from "Emotion Series: A Visual Journal."
Designed and pieced by Suzanne Evenson, photographed by Chas Krider.
"This quilt is a visual representation of my quest for peace and balance
in my life despite many uncertainties. . . . The center is filled with light.
It is a spiritual quilt."

THREADS OF REFLECTION

Centering Prayer

Relax and settle into your space. Close your eyes. When you are ready, pray repeatedly: "You, Holy One, are at my center."

Words of Scripture

In the morning, while it was still very dark, he got up and went out to a deserted place, and there he prayed.
—Mark 1:35

Quilt Reflections

Ponder the colors and design of Suzanne Evenson's quilt entitled "Journey to the Center" on page 80.

What does the quilt's design say to you?

Ponder how the quilt's design draws you into its center.

Sometimes we readily enter an experience of centeredness. Our spirits have been hungering for it, and our hearts rejoice at the opportunity.

Recall a time or a moment when you have known a sense of centeredness. What helps you to center? How would you describe the experience in your journal, in a quilt, or to a friend?

Sometimes, what we find at our center is tangled or confusing. If that has been your experience, take a moment to name the feelings you discern there. You might write about them in your journal, share what you can with someone you trust, or write a letter to God about those feelings.

Listening Prayer

I open my heart, God, to you and to the cares of your world. With what do you fill my heart?

COMPASSION

Clothe yourselves with compassion, kindness, humility,
meekness, and patience.

Colossians 3:12

THREADS OF TRADITION

Every day we are deluged with heartbreaking stories of war, senseless killings, natural disasters, and profound poverty around the globe. These crises seem overwhelming in their scope and depth. Our hearts quiver with the pain of these realizations. For many cultures around the world, quilting and handwork have provided an outlet for compassionate response to crises and tragedies.

Handwork provides an excellent form of tangible outreach. Creating quilts for fund-raising projects—church missions, social service needs, and disaster relief victims—is done widely throughout the United States. In addition, other quilters express compassion through quilts created specifically for groups with special needs. Quilts are given to children with life-threatening illnesses or to homeless populations living under a bridge. Though no funds are raised by these efforts, new connections are made that are the result of these caring acts.

8 2

Friendship or Signature Quilts

Shires Philathea Sunday School Class at the United Church of Christ in Salisbury, North Carolina, has been creating fund-raising quilts for many decades. One of the first was done in 1930–33 as a Dresden Plate configuration (a circular center with sculpted and wedge-shaped sections) with signatures of more than one hundred persons who paid to have their names sewn into the quilt. The profits from this shared project went to the church building fund. Typically, each woman who participated in making these friendship quilts would take responsibility for one or more blocks; she would ask family members and friends to donate a small sum—perhaps a dime or a quarter—for the privilege of having their names included on a block. Usually, the names were embroidered in spokes around the center of each block. The blocks were then put together by the women who had created them. The resulting quilt was either auctioned off, given to the minister, or offered to the person who had sold the most names.[1]

At-Risk Babies Crib Quilts

In a compassionate response to babies who were abandoned and dying of HIV in hospitals, Ellen Ahlgren began making quilts for these children in 1988. Once she became aware of the tragic circumstances of these little ones, her response was, "Well, what can you do for them besides make a quilt?" Within a year Ellen and her friend Ann White had founded the At-Risk Babies Crib Quilts, now known widely as the ABC Quilts organization, operated out of their home community in New Hampshire.[2]

There are now hundreds of coordinators across the country, and more than 200,000 of these little quilts. Each one is created with love. The quilts are distributed to infants with AIDS or born affected by alcohol, or shared with babies in neonatal and pediatric units and hospitals across the United States and around the world. They are given anonymously by quilters who send with them prayers and comfort for these tiny children suffering with these devastating problems.

Ahlgren believes that not only do these quilts comfort babies, but they help to educate and involve church groups and quilting bees about worldwide social issues.

Relief Auction for Worldwide Missions

Kidron, Ohio, is the scene every summer of the Mennonite Relief Auction. This event raises hundreds of thousands of dollars from the auction of extraordinarily beautiful handmade Mennonite and Amish quilts created by women's quilting groups in Holmes County, Ohio. These moneys are then put to use for worldwide Mennonite missions.

Quilt for the Cure

Susan was moved to create a quilt for a young woman who had been diagnosed with breast cancer. Susan has never met Stefanie, but as she heard more and more of Stefanie's story—a young mother with deep faith and hope for the future—she felt drawn to send her a warm quilt to surround her as she went through her treatments. Susan used fabrics that one design house had designated as Quilt for the Cure fabrics. Part of the funds from the sale of each bolt was given to research on breast cancer. Susan created a fresh log cabin design of blues, with yellow stars in the center, and lovingly mailed it to Stefanie with a prayer for her cure.

In addition to offering a unique form of compassion, outreach-quilting projects provide a vehicle for education and a real forum for addressing issues that individually we may feel are beyond our power to impact.

THREADS OF OUR SOULS

Compassion is the quivering of the heart in response to another's suffering.

Mary Jo Meadows[3]

When we are centered on our work, quilting is a form of compassion that feeds our own soul needs and provides warmth for others. Often going to the creative well of handwork fills up our empty bucket with hope and provides renewed energy to move forward. The restorative nature of quilting releases the quilt maker from being stuck in a quagmire of self-absorption or powerlessness. Often quilting provides the vehicle that carries us back up into the light where God might bring healing to our suffering and pain. Our own healing then provides the fuel that moves us beyond ourselves.

Compassion is at the heart of Christ's ministry. Christ was always moved by the stories of the downtrodden and those at society's margins. His healings emanated out of this deep "quivering of the heart" in the face of suffering. Joyce Rupp talks of compassion in her meditation book *The Cup of Our Life:* "Compassion is the quality of being able to get inside the skin of another in order to respond with loving concern and care."

We are all interconnected; therefore, when one suffers, we all suffer, just as when one rejoices, we all partake in the celebration. The more closely we are able to stay in the moment and remain aware of our connections, the more able we will be to respond with compassion. This is not an easy task. It is sometimes very painful to sit as a quiet witness to suffering while knowing that we are unable to change the course of that suffering.[4]

In order to abide being this type of witness, we must first care for ourselves. We must realistically assess our basic needs for emotional, creative, spiritual, and physical balance. Once we are anchored in an understanding of who we are, we are able to truly be present to the other.

We are also called to action when we see and know injustice is at the root of someone's suffering. "Spirituality is living an ordinary life in an extraordinary way with love [not fear] as the plumbline. Compassion requires action and sometimes confrontation." These are the challenging words of Rev. William Sloane Coffin in a lecture at First Community Church in Columbus, Ohio, in October 1998. Dr. Coffin advocates putting aside our fears and act out of our deepest knowing about justice. In the absence of justice, we must summon courage and act compassionately while naming and confronting the demons that plague our human existence. He cautions that this risk-taking behavior may cost ridicule and slander, but "compassion urges us to move out of our comfortable niches of security. Compassion stretches us and asks us to let go of apathy and indifference."[5]

Finally, we are encouraged, as Christ modeled for us on many occasions, to allow others to show their caring for us when we are suffering. Christ allowed him-

*"Warm Hands, Loving Heart," an ABC quilt created for babies at risk,
designed and quilted by Sue Powers. Each ABC quilt is signed "Love and comfort
to you" and given anonymously to critically ill babies in hospitals.*

self to be blessed by the love of his followers, to be anointed with precious oil and cared for by his community. This is sometimes the most difficult feature of compassion—accepting it on our own behalf.

Compassion, warmth, and love are quilted into many a quilt, arising from the depth of the maker's soul. Together, as members of quilting communities, we have the resources and creative energy to truly impact these issues and make a difference in the profile of our world. In addition to providing excellent and tangible means of outreach, quilt projects are vehicles for education and consciousness-raising about social justice issues.

THREADS OF REFLECTION

Centering Prayer

As I breathe in, I feel the quivering of my heart. As I breathe out, I send out compassion to all of creation.

Scripture

And if your neighbor cries out to me, I will listen, for I am compassionate.
—Exodus 22:26

Quilt Reflection

View the "Warm Hands, Loving Heart" quilt pictured on page 86.

How might your heart and hands work together in a compassionate way (e.g., cooking a warm meal for a lonely neighbor, knitting a pair of baby booties for an infant in an intensive care unit)?

What do you believe about service?

What sort of messages do you carry with you from your childhood or youth about caring for yourself and others?

Prayer

Teach me to find balance in my life, a balance that contains time with you and time for myself and others. May my prayers and actions be centered in your love and care for this world.

DISCIPLINE

Happy are those whom you discipline, O God,

and whom you teach out of your law.

Psalm 94:12

THREADS OF TRADITION

Piecing is the most popular process for quilt making. The pattern of a pieced quilt is created by cutting out pieces of a variety of fabrics and then sewing them together in new configurations to create the design. Before sewing machines, the simple running stitch used to hold together the hundreds of cloth pieces was done by hand, offering a repetitive activity that could be restful or relaxing at the end of a busy day. Today, many quilters still prefer the hand-sewn method, while others find that using a machine offers the same relaxation as well as the joy of creating more quilts in less time.

Quilters sometimes talk about "piecing our lives back together" as we are piecing a quilt. One quilt historian, writing about the early days of quilting in North America, describes how that restoration of ourselves may happen:

> Perhaps not so obviously, piecing a repetitive shape or unit restored a sense of order to life. It provided a retreat into an arranged, quiet world when there may have been no other way to find this. While furnishing stimulation through decisions as to the placement of color, the discipline of the pattern strengthened the sense of order as it provided definite parameters within which to work. Without conscious recognition, the very nature of these limits was reassuring.[1]

THREADS OF OUR SOULS

I (Susan) have thought and read much about women valuing ourselves, not giving ourselves away to everyone and everything until we are empty, with nothing left for ourselves or for God. I have often *felt* that emptiness, the stress that comes from realizing "I can't give anything to one more person today!" And the added stress of asking, "What have I *really* given? Has it been valuable at all?"

Quiet prayer time helps to nourish my soul, helps me reconnect to God and to myself, to my creative center. Quilting is often a part of the discipline of making time for prayer. That is especially true when quiet time is scarce or the discipline comes hard. When those times hit, I can sit at the sewing machine or quilt frame and know I am taking time for myself and for God. As I thread needles and set the frame, as I take first one stitch and then more, I feel myself begin to center. My spirit begins to settle in, to rest in God, in the rhythm of quilting, in the knowledge that I am making time for God and for myself. Chaos can be around me, but quilting begins to restore my soul, my center.

Valuing myself means taking time for myself. Time for myself means time with God, time with my creative center. Such time often includes reflections on my dreams, time for praying, healing, feeling, and imagining. Setting aside this time guarantees that I am also valuing the artist within and encourages the expression of my creativity, often evidenced in my quilting.

Many others have reflected on how the word "discipline" has negative connotations and overtones in our time and culture. So, some people prefer to use the word "practices" in reference to ways that we become more like the Holy One, for the times that we practice being the people of Christ we were called to be. Certain practices or habits will help us become more of who we were created to be. Both the word "disciple" and the word "discipline" share the same root meaning, which has to do with being taught and with practicing. Intentionally taking on certain practices—engaging in daily prayer, fasting, reading sacred texts, meeting with a spiritual friend or group of friends, or undertaking a host of other possibilities—will teach us more about ourselves and our God. Some intentionality and commitment to one's own growth are required.

In *Soul Feast*, Marjorie Thompson writes, "When it comes to spiritual growth, human beings . . . need structure and support. We need structure in order to have enough space, air, and light to flourish. Structure gives us the freedom to grow as we are meant to."[2] And she quotes William O. Paulsell, who said, "It is unlikely that we will deepen our relationship with God in a casual or haphazard manner. There will be a need for some intentional commitment and some reorganization in our own lives. But there is nothing that will enrich our lives more than a deeper and clearer perception of God's presence in the routine of daily living."[3]

Quilting is a daily activity and can be a discipline that leads me (Susan) to being more practiced in my prayer life. The time set aside for quilting helps me to affirm that I am *worth* the effort of taking time for my needs, my time with God, my expression of my creativity, my grounding for justice work.

Actually, quilting itself requires various disciplines: cutting, piecing, pressing, threading countless needles, basting, stitching, and binding. Of course, the same repetitive process that relaxes us can also be tedious on some days. Cutting out and then sewing together dozens upon dozens of small triangles can be boring, tedious to distraction. Sometimes—usually when I am pressed for time—I get to the point of wanting to toss out the project altogether and never see it again. In those moments, it is hard to remember the original inspiration or hoped for outcome. That is when true discipline is required, when I have to "practice" being patient, remind myself of the value of time apart from tasks and schedules, intentionally teach myself again the sacred significance of time for solitude.

I heard an experienced hand quilter say that in order to counteract boredom, she threads five needles a day and challenges herself to quilt until she has used them all. Another quilter, Suzanne Evenson, described arranging and rearranging the fabric pieces on a wallboard. She disciplined herself to live with the design a while, stand back from it, see it from different viewpoints, add to or take away colors, change the pattern, and leave it hanging for as long as it took until it was reflective of her creative imaginings and needs for expression.

Repetition, anticipation, reflection, remembrances—all represent aspects of spiritual practices. These "habits of the heart" have the potential to nurture our spiritual health and move us to incredible depths. They are habits that take us beyond the limitations of ourselves and require of us intentionality and openness. And when we are open, we just might receive something holy. Joyce Rupp wrote, "We need to value ourselves enough to spread our spiritual wings and receive God's energy."[4]

"Shaded Triangles," pieced and hand quilted by Bev Young.
This quilt depicts the patience and discipline required to work in
fine detail, with many small pieces.

THREADS OF REFLECTION

Centering Prayer

Choose a line from your favorite writing, from Joyce Rupp (above), or from a psalm or other passage of scripture, and go over it slowly, repeatedly, with your breathing.

Scripture

You are my Child, the Beloved; with you I am well pleased.
—Mark 1:11

Quilt Reflections

Enjoy and ponder Beverly Young's quilt on page 92.

Notice the pattern, the number of pieces in a block, the number of times a color or small unit repeats, and the way shading is accomplished.

How many hours would you guess were needed to make this quilt? Would making it have been tedious or relaxing for you?

What do you do that is relaxing, that makes time for yourself? For God? For appreciating the sacred in each day?

Write in your journal, or ponder with a friend, what you value about yourself.

What do you want to "practice" in your life?

Prayer

I know, God, that I belong to you, am loved by you. Bless my gifts, my yearnings to grow closer to you, and my efforts to value my sacred self. Amen.

· P R A Y E R ·

God will cover you with pinions,
and under God's wings you will find refuge.

Psalm 91:4

THREADS OF TRADITION

Prayer shawls have long been symbolic of being wrapped beneath the wings of God. A project has been growing called Cloak the Earth. "People of all faiths are coming together to make prayer cloths as tangible offerings of healing for the planet."[1] In November 1998 the retreat "Threads for Creativity" was held for the women of Park United Church of

Christ in Toledo, Ohio. Barb Davis and Marge Fenton, prayer partners in a spiritual direction program, led the women in the creation of a community prayer shawl. Each woman brought a precious piece of cloth from her life. Over the period of an evening and a day the women shared their sacred stories about the patches of cloth, and then the meditative process of creating a communal piece took place. Each woman shared a prayer about her life, and then they stitched, glued, and ironed on the patches of her life that would become the communal cloth binding their stories to one another.

Once the shawl was completed, the women were blessed as they passed underneath the cloth while reentering the space in which they had done their sharing. They then came together for eucharist and closing prayer led by their pastor, Rev. Joycelynn Degener. There was a mystical sense of being enveloped in the Holy throughout the creation of the shawl. Many women expressed during worship how powerful it was to combine their stories and prayers in that way. The shawl went home with a young mother of five whose husband had just been diagnosed with cancer. The prayer shawl is now a part of this community's prayer tradition.

THREADS OF OUR SOULS

As Louise Todd Cope, the creator of this prayer shawl idea, says,

> This process of making these tangible prayers elicits a dialogue. Questions that arise include What do we hold dear? How can we change our consciousness to become better stewards of the future? Can we envision our earth without the boundaries, which divide us and lead us on a journey of destruction? Our hope is that these prayer cloths can become metaphors of love cloaking pockets of the world that are torn and broken.[2]

The nightly news brings a constant barrage, indeed an onslaught, of incidents of violence, war, and abuses that we heap upon one another in our homes and communities. There is a major disconnect from Spirit in our modern lifestyles, fed by slick advertising that often promotes a disdain for and distance from the sacred. We rush breathlessly toward acquiring money and things. Work addiction and a thousand distractions deny the needs of our souls for quiet contemplation and play.

Two attitudes of prayer are contemplation and playful activities. Both serve as antidotes for the healing of our own souls and healing of our world. Recreation and quiet are two ways that we can express our hopes for our ailing planet. Balancing our daily responsibilities with prayer and leisure subdues our sense of being overwhelmed. The creative process can be the means through which we act out playfully what we come to know in contemplative prayer. Our intentionality in meditation and silence lets God know that we are open to the images and symbols that the Holy sets before us. It is this invitation to the Holy Spirit that then allows our inner creative urgings space for expression.

Besides this intentionality, our attitude about play will also dictate how available we are to the humorous nature of the Divine. Indeed, when we decide that we will and can be comfortable with playfulness and pleasure, we receive some unexpected messages from the Holy. Play that leads to pleasure is a vital resource for the growth of our souls. In our world laden with grief and sadness, pleasure becomes a significant counterpoint to pain. Thomas Moore writes, "When we begin to allow ourselves pleasure, our pain finds a context. . . . [Pain] becomes, not the focus of our lives, but just one aspect of living a life."[3] This implies not that we are to ignore the tragic flaws of our world, but that we must find creative ways of responding, ways that feed our own and others' souls as well.

One way to pray as we play that many quilters have discovered is to be immersed in the process of sewing a new creation. Sister Charlotte Trenkamp, or Sister Stitch as she is called by her quilting friends, said in the midst of a quilting retreat, "I feel like I am praying all day. Sometimes, I'm quiet. . . . I feel God is speaking to me."[4]

When we purposefully place ourselves in a receptive mode through our creative endeavors, we open ourselves to surprises from the Holy Creator. We allow God to speak to us in novel and unexpected avenues. Many quilters who shared their stories with us speak of quilting as prayer. Desiree Vaughn noted, "The process of designing and sewing, as well as the finished product, is a form of prayer. Although I attend church, this is a private time of worship."

Rev. Margaret Guenther, Episcopal priest, teacher, and director of the Center for Christian Spirituality in New York City, tells of a serendipitous error she made one day while journaling at her word processor. She wrote, "It will be necessary to play about that."

Guenther shares, "I am constantly struck by the proximity of 'play' and 'pray.' The linking of play and prayer and implicitly the linking of play with the work of contemplative living—is apparent in the mystical work *The Cloud of Unknowing*. That anonymous author shares that we are not 'at our spiritual best,' when we are struggling with our prayer life, we must still 'remain at it either in earnest or, as it were playfully.'"

Guenther likens this type of prayer to the childhood game of Hide and Seek: "There are times when we may feel forsaken or forgotten by God. We wonder if God is hiding or ignoring our pleas. It is especially at these times that we must remember that this prayer as play is like the game of 'Hide and Seek' or that of a playful parent God [who] is playing with us like a mother plays with her child. No sooner does the child look around and call for her than she runs back, arms outstretched, and embraces him."[5]

I (Barbara) had a similar incident recently. Over the past year as Susan and I have been writing this book, my husband and I have been going through some major life transitions. He has experienced unsettling developments in his career, which left us both feeling uncertain about the future. In addition, in an effort to downsize and simplify our life, we moved to a different home. We had been trying to sell our much-loved home of seven years for the past seven months. One Saturday in March when we were almost certain that the house had been sold, we received a call from our realtor that the deal had fallen through. Try as I might to relieve my anxieties about these changes and my disappointment over this new development, nothing seemed to help. My usual daily disciplines of scripture readings, prayer, and journaling seemed hollow and whiny. I felt that God was indeed hiding or certainly not providing obvious messages about why things were happening as they were in my life.

I turned to *Holy Listening,* Dr. Guenther's practical and very approachable book about spiritual direction. An immediate awareness came to me as I read her observations about the proximity of prayer and play. I remembered that prayer for me is an ongoing conversation with the Great Creative Spirit. Prayer is an elemental part of the creative process. I decided it was time to let go of my ruminations about our house and put play into my praying.

Playing with cloth to birth a new design can be an act of prayer. When one is aware that the Divine is guiding the process of creation at every step, there is a profound sense of a partnership, a Guiding Hand, and a readiness to receive a magnificent message from the Holy Other. Our praying and creating hands become God's resource as we determine how to embody what we are experiencing through the cloth patches.

I sprang into action as I realized that God was inviting me to play and pray my concerns out in a creative way. It was time to begin a quilt for our bed in our new home. Immersed once again in the promise of fresh new patterns in my life, I played as I gathered fabrics and searched for a design. By the end of my time that day with the new quilt project, I realized how hungry I had been to dip once again into the creative well, to dabble my fingers in the sweet honey pot of color and cloth. At the end of my play time I felt refreshed, less disquieted about the uncertainty in my life these days.

The next day, my husband and I drove out to check on our house. There was a knock at the door, and a delightful young couple told us that they had just discovered our house the previous day; they were in love with it and they intended to live in this house for a very long time.

"In God's Eyes," designed and quilted by Larry Nolan, S.J. A large circular piece that includes fabrics from around the globe, the quilt represents the artist's understanding of how God views our world.

THREADS OF REFLECTION

Centering Prayer

Holy Playmate, I search for you in every place, only to find that you have been waiting for me, even in the most obvious of places where I have forgotten to look. Help me to remember not to hide too well from you.

Scripture

So I tell you, whatever you ask for in prayer, believe that you have received it, and it will be yours. —Mark 11:24

Quilt Reflection

Sit with Father Larry's quilt on page 100. Father Larry sees God in all things and believes that "creativity is where God meets me." This hermit-priest recommends immersing ourselves in creative play as prayer.

Where have you sought the Creator? Where has the Creator met you?

Consider your daily activities. Make a list of the things that bring you a sense of fun or pleasure each day. Thank God for humor, whimsy, and laughter.

If this list is a difficult list to create, why not begin the next seven days by adding at least one activity that adds fun to your life?

Keep track of these activities in a journal.

At the end of seven days, review this list.

Do you have a sense of God at play with you?

Have you had a new awareness as a result of being intentional about playing?

Prayer

Often, God, when I am taking myself too seriously, you have a way of helping me to lighten up through peaceful, leisure activities. Thank you for the blessing of laughter, the excitement of new discoveries through the act of playing prayerfully and praying playfully.

GRIEF

So that you may not grieve as others do who have no hope.

I Thessalonians 4:13

THREADS OF TRADITION

Grief is one of the most profound experiences of being human. When mourning the loss of a loved one, we search for ways to keep their memory alive and to redefine who we are in their absence. Memory quilts have been used for generations to capture the preciousness of relationships now ended. "Clothing of the deceased person was pieced [into the quilts], as were ribbons and flowers from funereal wreaths."[1] In more recent times healing quilts of various types have been constructed to serve the same purpose: remembrance, as well as a way to process the loss.

Four brief contemporary stories in particular illustrate how God and the creative process of quilting help us to work through our losses. We have at our disposal creative and often inspired resources that we call upon to comfort ourselves during the saddest hours of our lives. Healing quilts are often done individually, as in Lesley Ann's story following her mother's sudden death. A seven-year-old child, Carli, remembers her dad in a quilt created during a support group at a cancer hospital. Many people join hearts and hands in community to make commemorative quilts such as the living quilt for AIDS victims. Some healing quilts document a serendipitous encounter with the Holy while working through loss, as in Barbara's dragonfly story.

THREADS OF OUR SOULS

Panels of Healing

Lesley Ann Hill is an art quilter who lives in Granville, Ohio. She was to have the first public show of her work at Columbus Cultural Arts Center in the fall of 1992. Her parents and grandmother were traveling to visit for the inaugural event when tragedy struck. Lesley Ann's mother and grandmother were killed in a car accident. She was devastated, and her initial reaction was one of guilt: "If they hadn't been coming to see my work, this accident would not have happened."

The creative juices were frozen in Lesley Ann's veins. Unable to disconnect her gifts as a quilter from the terrible loss of her mother, her best friend, Lesley Ann did not quilt for five years. Finally, she began to realize that her mother would not want her to suffer in this way. A drug and alcohol counselor, she knew that persons in recovery needed time to grieve the loss of their "best friend." Ritual is very important in dealing with loss.

Lesley Ann decided to ritualize her grief by creating a series of quilts about her reactions to this monumental loss. The results of this process were four quilted panels done in cotton. These four powerfully evocative panels, which were created over a one-year period, move through loss, anger, and depression to acceptance. At the completion of this series, Lesley Ann came to new awareness about gifts in her relationships with other family members still living. She also came to realize, "Mom will always be with me because I will love her forever."

In another quilt following this initial series which she called "In My Mother's Garden," Lesley Ann shares an image that came to her in a dream about her mother: "[This quilt] illustrates my concept that the place that we go after death is a marvelous place filled with light. It is comforting to know that even though my mother is not directly with us, she is in a wonderful place."

Carli's Memory Quilt

Verbal processing of grief is hard for adults and nearly impossible for a seven-year-old child. Quilting and other crafts offer healthy resources for the acknowledgment of our loss and allow us to represent in cloth what the loss has meant to us. Carli Shipley was only five years old when her dad was diagnosed with a brain tumor. Chuck struggled valiantly for two years through multiple treatment modalities to no avail.

The only child of Jana and Chuck Shipley, Carli was very much a part of the final weeks of home hospice care for her dad as he was dying. She and her mom were also involved in a support network at the James Cancer Hospital in Columbus, Ohio, called "Kids Can Cope." While in this support group, with help from mental health nurse facilitator Pauline King and quilter Martha Petrie, Carli created a memory quilt with pieces of her dad's jeans, pictures from favorite vacations, and a big heart that says "I Love You" for her dad. Carli keeps this treasure in a memory box with other gifts and mementos from her dad who died when she was six years old. When she needs comfort and misses her dad, Carli knows just where to find some solace. She goes to her memory quilt and to warm hugs from her family and friends. Carli shared that her quilt had traveled as far as Germany for a conference with Pauline, the nurse who had helped Carli when her dad died. Carli is very proud of her quilt and seemed pleased that her story was being shared with others.

Living Quilts

Hundreds of people across the United States were involved in bringing together quilt squares commemorating lives of loved ones fallen to the deadly AIDS virus. These quilts were laid end to end and side by side on the Mall in Washington, D.C., in the NAMES quilting project. Living quilts travel to many locations to remember victims of this horrendous disease. AIDS quilts have become important political and educational commentary as well as providing a much-needed memorial for the survivors. The living quilts raise awareness about the urgent need for increased research and medical support for those still struggling with a diagnosis of HIV and AIDS.

On Dragonflies and Other Winged Things (by Barbara Davis)

My brother, Mel, was twenty-seven years old when he died in a naval air crash on Catalina Island in 1969. I was unable to go to Mel's funeral as I was seven months pregnant with our first child, Jamie. Thus, I never had the opportunity to participate in a ritual of goodbye to my brother.

Twenty-seven years after Mel's death I went to San Diego with my husband, Terry. After being lost in San Diego, I serendipitously found the military cemetery where Mel is buried. The miles of singular white icons in that cemetery—Christian crosses, Stars of David, and other religious representations—overtook me. After a long search, I found Mel's grave. It was there that I came to a real sense of closure as I sat and prayed. I remembered Mel; remembered, too, our relationship with its struggles and gifts. A new realization gripped me as I contemplated what it means now to have a son of my own who is just the age Mel was when he died.

I left the cemetery renewed and with a wish that I could find a symbol of my visit with Mel to take home to Mom and Dad. In a small outdoor shopping area I found a pleasant young man selling jewelry. I spied a delightful dragonfly pin in jade green and brilliant blues. I took this home with me from this beautiful place with plans to give it to Mom for Mother's Day.

The morning after we returned from our trip, I sat down at our computer to do some work. I discovered the most amazing and synchronistic story written by our friend Howard Friend, a Presbyterian minister, on our word processor. Howard and my closest friend, Betsy Friend, had been to visit us a few weeks before we left for California. Howard had used some of that time to work on his recently published book *Recovering the Sacred Center* about the healing needed in our church institutions. The following is a condensed version of what Howard left on our word processor:

> Cecil B. DeMille had lost his wife and was in deep mourning. One day as he floated alone on a small rowboat on a quiet pond in Maine . . . a water beetle had wandered up the side of the old wooden boat. . . . Cecil simply gazed at the beetle. . . . Then the water beetle seemed to shudder and to lurch and . . . it rolled on its side and died! DeMille felt a fresh stirring of grief for his wife, now mingled with the death of his new

acquaintance. . . . The better part of an hour passed. Suddenly, the water beetle seemed to stir . . . it was moving. The husk cracked and fell away . . . emerging from the husk was a dragonfly.[2]

The dragonfly has since become a symbol of new life for my family and me. Sharing the dragonfly pin and this story with my parents was a healing moment for all of us.

Just this year I found the most wonderful bright pink print with a riot of colorful greens, purples, and yellows and whimsical dragonflies throughout the pattern. I made an "Around the World" baby quilt with the print. As I created this lively little piece, I prayed that the birth of a new child into this world would bring a renewed sense of hope and resurrection for yet another family.

*"In My Mother's Garden" by Lesley Ann Hill. Designed and pieced
with machine embroidery, hand appliqué, and beading by Lesley Ann.
The idea for the quilt came to her in a dream about her mother,
who had died in a car accident.*

THREADS OF REFLECTION

Centering Prayer

Hidden God, you know my deepest wounds and most profound grief. Be with me as I seek to find healing and a sense of new life in all that happens.

Scripture

So that you may not grieve as others do who have no hope. For since we believe that Jesus died and rose again, even so, through Jesus, God will bring with him those who have died.
— 1 Thessalonians 4:13–14

Quilt Reflection

Look at Lesley Ann Hill's quilt "In My Mother's Garden" on page 108. How do you feel as you view this quilt?

The stories in this chapter are meant as witnesses to resurrection and new life. They are all stories of loss, but each led to a creative outlet for expression of the feelings related to the loss.

Think of your own losses.

What ways have you found to commemorate loved ones and your feelings about your relationship?

Do you have any symbols that give you hope or a sense of new life? If none come to mind, think about ones that you might like to adopt in nature: a flower, a special tree.

Make a note of special symbols in your journal.

Watch for the occurrence of these symbols in your ordinary experience.

When they occur in your life, say a prayer of thanks for the reminder that God is ever present in all that happens in our lives.

Prayer

I give thanks for healing gardens, for dragonflies, and for all the reminders that you walk through all of the passages of my life, O God.

JOY

You have turned my mourning into dancing; . . .
and clothed me with joy.

Psalm 30:11

THREADS OF TRADITION

For many quilters, a certain joy comes from being around fabric. Whenever I (Susan) am sad or depressed, I can count on a trip to the fabric shop to lighten my mood. As I am encircled by countless color variations and endless pattern designs, the combinations of texture, color, and design seem infinite. There are yet more quilts to be designed and made! Inspiration may strike as I study and enjoy a new line of fabric, leaf through a pattern book, or engage in conversation with another quilter. Although I am as ravenous as the next quilter when it comes to adding to my stash of fabric, I don't even need to purchase any to experience the frequent enchantment of being surrounded by cloth. Seeing certain colors nurtures the soul, imagining quilt designs unleashes creativity, and experiencing varieties of textures calls forth memories and dreams.

In his delightful book *Cloth and Comfort*, Roderick Kiracofe comments on the joyful connection between women and fabric: "Just as quilting parties brightened a pioneer woman's social circle, the quilts themselves—sometimes even mere swatches of cloth tucked into a letter—became the talismans of old friends and loved ones who were far away."[1]

Women and men often quilt and create art in solitude, yet as Kiracofe and others suggest, the times around the quilt frame offer another joy—the joy of companionship and the delight of a shared passion. Classes in quilt making, art, and design offer opportunities for community enjoyment. While more and more quilts are quilted by machine today, reflecting the fast pace of our lives perhaps, quilting classes seem to replace the quilting frame in some respects. Not as many women gather as regularly around a quilt frame to work on one person's quilt, so time together in a class provides welcomed occasions for bonding, even if it is in a more limited time frame. By whatever process—fabric, bee, or class—the hope and celebration of our lives spill over into our quilts.

THREADS OF OUR SOULS

Joy and sorrow, hope and despair are intertwined in life. Around the quilting frame, women have shared their experiences of the highs and lows of life. Together they cry, laugh, joke, reprimand, encourage, exchange wisdom and recipes, teach, and console one another. And in the midst of it all, a quilt emerges—something warm and healing, something extraordinary out of the ordinary stuff of life, something from the fabrics we enjoy and may have worn previously. Besides the pleasure of creating a work of art, the joy and celebration mentioned by other quilters were not exclusively about the quilt itself or the creative process. Time and again, they found the most remarkable joy in the relationships, the friendships that grew and were enriched over time.

A group of North Carolina quilters, used to meeting in a local adult recreation center, wrote to us about a gathering they held for the sole purpose of discussing the questionnaire we had developed around quilting and spirituality. Eloquently, Norma Zunich, a visitor to the group, wrote about that gathering:

Perhaps the most important observation from this gathering was the emerging realization of how much these women mean to each other. They live in different neighborhoods, pursue different careers, and attend different churches. Their "quilting life" was somewhat compartmentalized. This was the first time they had met at a member's home. They giggled over how they'd marked time by their children's rites of passage and by the birth of grandchildren. Together they offered each other strength through difficult times, including the sudden death of a son, the lingering death of a daughter-in-law, and a severe stroke of one member. Comments surfaced such as: "I would not be who I am nor where I am without this group and without my quilting." "We're all better people because of each other. We are helpful to each other. We learn how to live from each other." One woman quietly reflected that this quilting group is a "cornerstone in our lives." As the discussion was ending, all agreed that "they would feel unfulfilled without the richness and meaning quilting and quilting friendships have brought them."[2]

Just before Christmas one year, a newsletter arrived from our local quilt and stained glass shop. The owners, Bev and Gary Young (quilt artist and stained glass artist, respectively), shared their reflections about beginning their twentieth year as founders and owners of this unique shop, the Glass Thimble:

Once in a great while, we have conjured up a truly original idea, but, as we talked, we were struck with the realization that the lion's share of good ideas and great experiences have been an outgrowth of the relationships and friendships formed with those who entered our door. . . . When we looked back at 19 years of really hard work and some significant successes, both of us found ourselves reciting remembrances of thoughts shared with this person, things done with that person. Most of the important memories came with a name (or names) attached, memories that included other people who somehow miraculously joined us in this amazing carousel ride. . . . It may be that the heart of any business is to make a profit, but if a business has a soul, it is defined by the friendships fashioned over the years.[3]

So many things happen around quilting, whether in the quilt shop, or around the table at a quilt class, or in the midst of a quilting bee. Many of those happenings are cause for celebration. At least two of those happenings worth celebrating are deeply spiritual: the connection to others and the connection to self. Wendy Bynner, a quilter in Ohio, describes her profound joy at the connections to other women that quilting brought her:

> As an associate professor of veterinary radiology, I spent most of my adult life in a profession that, at least initially, had very few women in it. Now, since I retired in 1995, I find that quilting helps me connect to other women—all of my close friends are quilters and I belong to several monthly groups related to quilting. Quilting has become an all-consuming passion for me. I enjoy working with all the beautiful fabric we have available now and making things for people I know, as well as for charitable organizations. So, quilting connects me to the past and to other women in the present. It also helps me express my spirituality and gratitude to God for all of the abundant blessings I have enjoyed in my life. I can't imagine my life without being able to quilt.[4]

Wendy's words articulate well the joy that quilting brings to many of us as we discover ourselves, our friendships, our commitments, and a deep sense of the Holy around our shared passion.

In the middle of a quilting class or group of friends, with eight to ten women gathered around a table, I (Susan) am frequently struck by how we birth ourselves there. Most of us listen intently to one another, and in that listening, we learn more about our own lives, our own souls. In *Women's Ways of Knowing*, Mary Belenky and others comment on how women grow in self-understanding: "Women typically approach adulthood with the understanding that the care and empowerment of others is central to their life's work. Through listening and responding, they draw out the voices and minds of those they help to raise up. In the process, they often come to hear, value and strengthen their own voices and minds as well."[5]

When we so frequently feel excluded from other arenas of life, circles of women—whether they are new friends or old—listen one another into a journey of self-discovery. Sometimes without even realizing it, our shared conversations and insights propel another person several steps farther along that eternal journey toward wholeness, a journey that claims our inherent holiness every step of the way. I often look at the other quilters gathered around me and think of Henri Nouwen's remarkable discovery of radiance in every human being. After having spent months in a monastery, seeing the same people day after day, he left for a brief visit to a local dentist and, upon walking down a crowded street, was struck by the joyful observation that people "walk around shining like the sun."[6]

For many of us who gather around quilting frames and tables, glimpses of the Holy in the eyes of others are analogous to sacred glimpses captured around other tables, especially the communion table or the Seder meal. Around the many tables of our lives, we listen to one another, we hear sacred stories, we give thanks for the wonder of the giftedness of life, we express our outrage at societal injustices, we inspire one another to work for justice and peace, and we celebrate the joy of God's love for us. In so doing, we move deeper into our own true selves, the persons God created us to be. That movement inward also has the frequent effect of launching us outward, beyond ourselves, into action with and on behalf of others. Quilters around the world have joined together to create ABC quilts for at-risk babies and have made and auctioned thousands of quilts in hundreds of churches to raise money for causes far beyond their own walls. As recently as April 1999, following the news report of a child freezing to death, the World Wide Quilters Web Page invited quilters to donate Kosovo Quilts to be sent to refugee children in that war-torn area. The compassion born of friendship, of inner work, soul work, and contemplation, does not stop with the self, but blossoms into deep empathy and action. Such is the joy of quilters, summed up for us by quilter Barb Sills: "[Quilting] has been the only pastime that has combined four features important to me: meeting people, learning, service to others, and fun."

A Columbus, Ohio, quilter, Desiree Vaughn described for us the joy of quilting: "When I am quilting, I am the happiest, which to me means I'm doing what I was meant to do. When people make things . . . they leave a part of their soul or spirit in that item. When I stroke the old quilts that have been made by women of the family and handed down generation to generation, I can *feel* their presence or spirit. There is a connection between the past and present."

When people act on their own joy and compassion, they have a sense of empowerment and a greater sense of hope about the future. One may think, "I have done what I can do. I have contributed toward alleviating a crisis or a problem." That sense of hope spills over into the often quiet joy of creating a personal legacy. Desiree Vaughn expressed it this way: "Since I do not have children of my own, I'm hoping some of my work will be here after I am gone, just to show I really was here. My nieces and nephews are going to have a lot of quilts!" Pamela Hardiman, a quilter living in Connecticut, expressed her aspirations for the future with these words: "I hope I will be able to spread my ideas about using quilts as processional banners and inspire others to make quilts for worship communities. I hope my example of working diligently with fabric for so many years will inspire others and give them hope, pass hope on like a flame."

These hopes of quilters, their compassion and their dreams, their fears and their sorrows, are all stitched into their quilts. Like other sacred symbols in our lives, quilts touch our spirits because they are invested with meanings and traditions that remind us where we come from and who we are as people. Since God is compassionate, feel-

"Rainbow Quilt," an original design by Susan Shie, pieced and quilted by James Acord and Susan Shie. The purpose of the quilt, one of a series of "Green Quilts" by these artists, is to raise awareness about the needs of our environment.

ing our pains, our wounds, and our sufferings, we are being and acting in the image of the One who created us when we express compassion and hope, when we share joy.

THREADS OF REFLECTION

Centering Prayer

Hold or wrap around you a quilt or other sacred object. As you still yourself, repeat the following prayer with the rhythm of your breathing: "Your hope resides within me."

Scripture

I often boast about you; I have great pride in you; I am filled with consolation; I am overjoyed.
—2 Corinthians 7:4

Quilt Reflection

Enjoy the colors, the design, and the many intricate details and writing on the quilt on page 116.

About this quilt, quilt artist Susan Shie says, "The quilt is all about our lives, centered in our Rainbow Garden. It's a celebration of the joy in making a garden, and in keeping oneself grounded to Earth, through the tasks of making things grow."[7]

What expressions of joy do you find in this quilt?

Reflect on or record in your journal an experience of joy from your own life. What was that experience like?

What design or symbol would express that feeling of joy for you?

How might you use colors and cloth to express joy?

Prayer

God of Joy and of Dancing,

Bless our moments of celebration and joy. May we be more and more connected to you, our source of joy, hope, and compassion. May we be more and more connected to our ancestors, our family and friends, our world, ourselves. Out of those connections, may we grow in joy and hope. Amen.

APPENDIX: Quilters' Stories

Many of the stories and reflections that we received from quilters are interwoven into the preceding chapters. In the following pages, however, several quilters speak for themselves, in their own voices. Their stories encompass the wide range of passions, commitments, motivations, and reflections on the art of quilting and spirituality that is representational of all the stories that we were privileged to receive. We offer them in honor of all quilters.

CHRISTINE PORTER'S STORY

I retired as a public school speech and language pathologist in June 1994. Finding myself alone after thirty years of marriage, I knew I must explore latent interests. I have been a sewer since my grandma Sarah first taught me to make doll clothes at age ten. I have continued to love fabrics: the textures, the colors, the designs, the complements of it all. I made a few patchwork pillows before I retired, but no major work.

In October 1994, I discovered Donna Slusser and Pat Magaret's book *Watercolor Quilts*. Since I had just completed two watercolor (with brushes) classes at our nighttime adult vocational school, I read the book quite thoroughly and proceeded to gather quarter-yard pieces of fabric and cut two-inch squares out of them. I now have six wall-hanging examples, two of which were accepted at the juried Youngstown, Ohio, Women Artists Celebration (May 1998). This was indeed an honor for me. Only 131 of 340 works were accepted.

The pieces are no longer typical watercolor examples, although I continue to use the two-inch square technique. Rather, they have become symbols of love and expressions of nature. Several times people have expressed independently, without prompting, about how spiritual they are.

[Quilting] is truly a spiritual experience for me. I often feel that as I work, what is transformed to my work board is not done by me, but through me. I am only the hand. What appears is surely the Holy Spirit's leading. I do not pretend the projects are perfect . . . rather they are my best at this time as guided by God. There is such peace in this, such fulfillment, such a long-needed feeling of self-worth. I am now able to accept that what I have constructed has value. Of all the things I've done and made in sixty-two years of living, this is truly amazing to me. I will always give thanks for this blessing.

There is so much more to tell you: how I received the questionnaire for this book, the rediscovery of lost friends, the encounters with truly gifted, creative, amazing women, development of new friendships, healing of strained relationships. Coincidence? I believe it's all part of the Holy Spirit helping me heal and put order to my life. Perhaps even giving me new life.

Grandma would be so proud of me. Her quilts and threads on wooden spools and buttons decorate my workroom.

KITTY TOWNER'S STORY: "MY M AND M QUILT"

Over sixty-eight years ago, my mother, Mildred A., and her friend Mildred S. collected pieces of cotton prints to make a colorful quilt in the Dresden Plate pattern on white muslin squares. My birth halted the production. The partially finished squares were rolled and stored in a brown bag in the hot attic. Once or twice they were laid out to admire, then rolled again and put into a new brown bag. Still unfinished, they ended up, all loose and mixed up, in the bottom drawer of a sewing cabinet, under scraps of more recent projects.

My interest in quilting has grown in the past few years. When Mildred A. was homebound with a broken ankle, I thought of the muslin squares and the Dresden Plates. I carefully washed the completed squares, which came up with very few rust spots and none the worse for the long delay. New muslin was used to hold the loose "plates," and my mother outlined them with embroidered buttonhole stitch so they all would match. The knowledgeable women at the quilt fabric shop were excited to see the old patterns of the cotton pieces. We picked out the lashing material and the floral print for the border and the back.

I machine stitched the nine squares into a twin-size quilt. The tenth square I made into a pillow for Mother, Mildred A., for her birthday. It looks comfortable in her home. I started hand quilting the quilt, but I knew it would take me many more years to complete. So the women at a Wilmington Presbyterian Church beautifully hand quilted my nine-square muslin M and M quilt. I sewed the muslin binding by hand and am ready to show it off. Mother was pleased with the completed project that she and Mildred S. started so long ago. It will be handed down to one of my daughters.

BARB SILL: "QUILTING—MY NEW BEST FRIEND"

I first learned to sew in high school, mostly out of necessity so I could have new clothes. Finding that I enjoyed it, I later made my own wedding dress, sewed Easter dresses and Christmas jumpers for my two daughters when they were little, and stitched numerous decorating projects around our house. From time to time I've cross-stitched, needlepointed, crocheted, and embroidered. But nothing—nothing— has captured me like quilting. Primarily machine quilting.

I'm probably still viewed as a novice, having only learned to quilt three years ago. But it seems as comfortable as being with an old friend. It has been the only pastime that has combined four features important to me: meeting people, learning, service to others, and fun. I first got involved in quilting through a volunteer project—Team Battelle ABC Quilters—where I worked. Many of us joined this project not even knowing how to quilt, but we had a strong desire to learn. After several classes where we learned the basics, we were turned loose to work in groups or individually as long as we fulfilled their mission of making quilts that would be donated to hospitals around Ohio that cared for AIDS-infected and other high-risk babies. I was hooked.

I met people I'd never known where I worked. I recruited several friends to join me, one of whom was having difficulty facing a personal problem, and set out the first year to make twelve quilts. We are all addicted now. I continue to make quilts for ABC Quilters, but also have found time to make quilts for my family, friends, fund-raisers, and for myself.

Quilting was one of the reasons I went into my supervisor one day about a year ago and resigned from a twenty-five-year career. I had been the supervisor for all volunteer projects with that company.

A bold move, but I had begun to realize I needed to bring more balance into my personal life, and this was one sure way to do that. I have never regretted that decision.

My new best friend has brought me hours of joy, helped me meet new people, and provided a new outlet to serve those in need. And I am constantly learning new techniques and new designs. Even when I'm alone I never feel lonely now that I have learned to quilt.

Isn't that what friends are for?

LILA BREWER'S STORY: "SURVIVAL"

It took me almost a lifetime to discover quilting! I was nearly eighty years of age when I decided to take a course at the local high school. After taking the course, a small group of friends joined together to comfort, console, and aid each other as we hoped to become adept, experienced quilters. We started with an easy table runner, but I soon ventured forth, in my ignorance, to attempt a queen size (which became a king size!) "Around the World" quilt. Since I was making the quilt for my daughter, Barb, and her husband, Terry, she joined me in the project. We found it challenging, but a real revelation when we went to choose colors and fabric. We soon became "hooked" on color and design. For me, that was a spiritual experience—a closeness that developed in discovering each other's tastes and choices. The same closeness and joy became apparent when our other daughter, Scottie, and I chose colors and fabrics for a quilt for her Vermont home. With each daughter, the discoveries we made together were a natural extension of already close relationships and definitely a spiritual bonding. The quilts will be a reminder of our love for one another and, hopefully, a legacy for our children and our grandchildren.

My fabric collage was created at the time when I was receiving radiation treatments for breast cancer, during May and June 1997. Later the quilt was accepted in a juried show at New Britain Museum of American Art, in a show entitled "Art for the Cure." It was an American Cancer benefit.

To me, the fabric collage was a form of meditation and a time of relaxation as I stitched. In contemplating the piece later, it spoke of darkness, showing a limiting space around two central, vulnerable figures. And yet, there are glimpses of light and beauty in the brightening at the fringes and in the peaceful landscape at one side— visions of hope and serenity reaching beyond fear and uncertainty.

Now, one year beyond the cancer for me, and five years beyond our daughter Scottie's cancer—we are survivors. I am thankful for research, treatment, and prayers.

JANET RICHARDSON'S STORY

The church that I attend has been my family's choice for generations. David's Church in Canal Winchester, Ohio, has a quilting group called the Cinderellas, traditionally a group of retired women who get together every Tuesday morning and make quilts. They break for a brown-bag lunch at noon, then continue quilting into the afternoon. Their goal is a quilt for everyone who has been hospitalized, newborns, and/or baptisms. They have printed fabric labels with the recipient's name and the name of the group and the group's well wishes. The Cinderellas fund this operation and other special projects to meet the needs of the church.

I have firsthand experience of watching the face of a recipient of the Cinderellas' group gift, seen a face light up at receiving such a thoughtful gift, one that "blankets" them with warmth and affection. The quilt is tangible proof that prayers have been said for them and continues a sense of community and belonging.

After my children were through with the baby stages, I kept their receiving blankets, which were all high-grade cotton flannel. I cut them and fitted them together, intermingling printed and solid blocks. While I never backed it, I use it for a lap robe on cold winter evenings. Touching that flannel fabric always reminds me of the way I felt holding and nurturing my children as babies. The fabric is faded, stained, and yet I always smile and feel "warmed" when I see it. I am so glad I preserved both the flannel and the feelings.

I believe that gifts of quilting are much more than just an object. They are an affirmation that someone took considerable time and thoughtfulness to remember you.

CAROL VASENKO'S STORY

Quilting is my way of sharing and connecting. I view designing as my creative expression of spirituality. I am constantly thinking about what I can create, seeing creativity as at least approaching spirituality.

I like art, and use fabric as a medium. The act of designing is, for me, a balm; very soothing. I don't particularly like hand quilting; I like the dreaming-up-the-idea part best of all. In that place where I am thinking up ideas, I heal.

I don't "quilt" in the traditional sense at all. I make fabric collages, based, I hope, on the principles of any art form. I just happen to use fabric instead of paint. I dye, print, paint my own fabrics, and use my own designs. Currently I am working on a wall hanging depicting Alzheimer's disease, and am enrolled in an online project to create wall hangings having something to do with the horrors of child abuse. I feel very strongly about this issue, but have no clue about how to present this idea on fabric! I am mulling it over. Although I do make decorative quilts to hang above the proverbial couch, I have been more interested in making visual statements about some concern I have, or sometimes merely to show that even the ordinary can become extraordinary.

BARBARA EMERY'S STORY

I started quilting in the late '50s. I had no idea how to go about it. My Scottish ancestry and New England upbringing made it a natural hobby for me, as it encompasses creating something useful and beautiful out of fabrics that I already have on hand. My first project was covering old chairs with wool patches, feather stitching them directly onto the old material. It was an especially hard time in my life and the therapy of doing this saved my sanity. I also made a crib quilt using very tiny triangular pieces. It really is a very unique "crazy quilt."

When an evening quilting class was offered at our high school I said "this is for me." Out of that class, a number of us formed the Bicentennial Quilt Club. We had many years of sharing, laughing, traveling to quilt shows, helping and admiring each other's handiwork and enjoying the camaraderie. I made bed quilts, wall hangings, and pillows for my grandchildren. Whoever sleeps in the beds in our home is kept warm with my handiwork. We made a group quilt—each person making a different red, white, and blue square. For a while, the quilt was displayed in our municipal center.

As time went on, the club disbanded. I tried counted cross-stitch and other crafts. Nothing really touched me until last fall when my oldest granddaughter asked me to help her with "snuggle quilts" for her three kids for Christmas. She's a very busy mom, so I offered to do them myself. My husband and I have ten great-grandchildren and three young grandchildren who spend a lot of time together. The kids who already have their quilts carry them for "overnights." I was plagued with a vision problem for five months that prevented me from driving. I was able to sew and do things around the house, however. Working on those quilts helped me through the winter.

Since my fingers aren't as nimble as they once were, I no longer do pieced or complicated patterns, but I can do patchwork, tied quilts on the machine. I'm never more content or at peace than when I'm cutting out the eight-inch squares, arranging them so they are pleasing to the eye and, of course, in colors that the children have selected to match their rooms. As I sort the colors (I especially love that part), arrange them, and sew them together to form the top, then layer it with fluffy batting and the backing, I think about each child—their personalities, their interests, and how much I love them and I pray that they will lead healthy, happy lives. My husband and I have been blessed with a large family—thirty-four of us right now and one grandchild and one great-grandchild on the way. My work is cut out for me.

SUSAN SHIE'S STORY

Susan Shie is an art quilter who collaborates on her work with husband James Acord. Susan has a sense of urgency about the failing health of our earth's environment. She is also deeply passionate about world peace and justice. Her art quilts are her voice, her narrative about these issues. Her passion led to the creation of a quilt she calls "Home Sweet Home." Susan began a worldwide effort in 1991 to awaken others to the need to speak out about social justice and environmental issues. Susan urges, "Let people all over the world make quilts that say something positive about the environment. Let them put their prayers or affirmations of healing into that work."

Another piece by Susan is called "Earth Quilt." This is one of a series about the four basic elements—earth, fire, water, and air. In this quilt Susan combines her grief over the killing of four students at Kent State University in May 1970 with her belief in the need for daily rituals to care for our planet and one another.

NOTES

INTRODUCTION

1. Mary Bywater Cross, "Quilts from the Mormon Trail," *American Patchwork and Quilting* (June 1998): 8.

ART

1. Ruth H. Roberson, ed., *North Carolina Quilts* (Chapel Hill: University of North Carolina Press, 1988), 6.

2. Kenneth T. Lawrence, ed., *Imaging the Word: An Arts and Lectionary Resource*, vol. 1 (Cleveland: United Church Press), 10.

3. Poakalani and John Serrao, *The Hawaiian Quilt: A Spiritual Experience* (Honolulu: Mutual Publishing, 1997), 10–11.

4. Sue Bender, *Plain and Simple: A Woman's Journey to the Amish* (New York: HarperCollins, 1989), 78–79.

5. Susan A. Blain, ed., *Imaging the Word: An Arts and Lectionary Resource*, vol. 2 (Cleveland: United Church Press), 76.

6. Serrao, *The Hawaiian Quilt*, 60.

STORYTELLING

1. Carolyn Mazloomi, *Spirits of the Cloth: Contemporary African-American Quilts* (New York: Clarkson Potter, 1998), artist's statement, 182.

2. Carolyn Mazloomi, quoted from *Unraveling the Stories: Quilts as a Reflection of Our Lives*, videotape by Luanne C. Bole-Becker (Cleveland: B. B. Sound & Light Ltd., 1997).

3. Quoted in Anne Simpkinson, Charles Simpkinson, and Rose Solari, eds., *Nourishing the Soul: Discovering the Sacred in Everyday Life* (San Francisco: Harper San Francisco, 1995), 187.

4. Jacqueline Tobin and Raymond G. Doubard, *Hidden in Plain View: A Secret Story of Quilts and the Underground Railroad* (New York: Doubleday, 1999), 187.

5. Susan A. Blain, ed., *Imaging the Word: An Arts and Lectionary Resource*, vol. 2 (Cleveland: United Church Press), 40.

6. Tina Battock, "Quilting in America 1997," *Quilters Newsletter*, (spring 1998).

7. Daphne Taylor, "On the American Quilt: Reflections of a Quilter," *Mother Earth News* (December–January 1999), 14.

FINDING OUR VOICES

1. Roberson, *North Carolina Quilts*, 161.

2. Ibid., 162.

3. Cathleen R. Bailey, as quoted in *Spirits of the Cloth*, 175.

4. K. Wind Hughes and Linda Wolf, *Daughters of the Moon, Sisters of the Sun: Young Women and Mentors in the Transition to Womanhood* (British Columbia, Can., and New Haven, Conn.: New Society Publishers, 1997), 1–2.

5. Ibid., 2.

6. Sister Carol Ann Spencer, Wellstreams class, Columbus, Ohio, 1998.

7. Kerry Hoffman, ed., *Erika Carter: Personal Imagery in Art Quilts* (Bothell, Wash.: Fiber Studio Press and That Patchwork Place, 1996), 12.

8. Laurie Bushbaum, "Woman of the Cloth," *Art Quilt Magazine*, no. 9 (1998): 19.

9. Roland L. Freeman, *A Communion of the Spirits: African-American Quilters, Preservers, and Their Stories* (Nashville: Rutledge Hill Press, 1996), 155.

CREATIVITY

1. Matthew Fox, *Original Blessing: A Primer in Creation Spirituality, Presented in Four Paths, Twenty-Six Themes, and Two Questions* (Santa Fe: Bear & Company, 1983), 185.

2. Susan Gordon Lydon, *The Knitting Sutra: Craft as a Spiritual Practice* (New York: Harper-Collins, 1997), 139.

3. Ibid., 138.

4. Sue Bender, *Everyday Sacred: A Woman's Journey Home* (San Francisco: Harper San Francisco, 1995), 6.

IMAGES OF GOD

1. Miriam Schapiro, "A Woman's Way," *Art Quilt Magazine*, no. 9 (1998): 32.

2. Ibid.

3. Sausalito, Calif., Institute of Noetic Science, *Noetic Sciences Review* (winter 1997). Inside cover photograph of a painting by Lee Lawson.

MYSTERY

1. Anthony De Mello, S.J., *The Song of the Bird* (New York: Doubleday, 1984), 98.

2. Dawn Gibeau, "Pieces and Patterns of Our Lives," *Praying* (Kansas City: The National Catholic Reporter Publishing Company), no. 91 (1 March 1999): 8.

3. Ibid., 6.

4. Margaret Miller, *Strips that Sizzle* (Bothell, Wash.: That Patchwork Place, 1992).

COMMUNITY

1. Roberson, *North Carolina Quilts*, 52.
2. Ibid., 63.
3. Ibid., 64.
4. As quoted by Mazloomi, *Spirits of the Cloth*, 144.
5. Ibid.
6. Gibeau, "Pieces and Patterns of Our Lives," 5, 29.
7. Ibid., 8.

HEALING

1. Pat Maixner Magaret and Donna Ingram Slusser, *Watercolor Impressions: Quilts Inspired by the Best Seller Watercolor Quilts* (Bothell, Wash.: That Patchwork Place, 1995).
2. Bushbaum, "Woman of the Cloth," 18.
3. Larry Dossey, *Beyond Illness: Discovering the Experience of Health* (Boulder, Colo.: New Science Library, 1985).

FORGIVENESS

1. Freeman, *A Communion of the Spirits*, 129.
2. Ibid.
3. Ibid., 131.

LIBERATION

1. Tobin and Doubard, *Hidden in Plain View*, a paraphrase of Mrs. Williams reporting on the Quilt Code.
2. Nancy Callahan, *The Freedom Quilting Bee* (Tuscaloosa: University of Alabama Press, 1987), 24–25.
3. Ibid., 29.

CENTERING

1. Serrao, *The Hawaiian Quilt*, 15.
2. Ibid., 17.
3. Ibid., 19.

COMPASSION

1. Quoted in Joyce Rupp, *The Cup of Our Life: A Guide for Spiritual Growth* (Notre Dame, Ind.: Ave Maria Press, 1997), 110.
2. Roberson, *North Carolina Quilts*.
3. Lois Shea, "Awareness: A Side Benefit to AIDS Quilts," *Boston Sunday Globe*, 31 July 1994, "Granite Chips."

4. Rupp, *The Cup of Our Life*, 110.

5. Rev. Dr. Wm. Sloane Coffin, lecture at First Community Church, Columbus, Ohio, October 1998.

DISCIPLINE

1. Roberson, *North Carolina Quilts*, 99.

2. Marjorie J. Thompson, *Soul Feast: An Invitation to the Christian Spiritual Life* (Louisville: Westminster John Knox Press, 1995), 137.

3. William O. Paulsell, as quoted in *Soul Feast*, 137.

4. Rupp, *The Cup of Our Life*, 34.

PRAYER

1. Louise Todd Cope, introduction to handout provided at the "Cloak of Protection for the Earth" workshop held in Utah, May 1999 (Cloak the Earth Project, Berkeley, Calif., photocopy).

2. Ibid.

3. Thomas Moore, "The Art and Pleasure of Caring for the Soul," in *Nourishing the Soul*, 18.

4. Gibeau, "Pieces and Patterns of Our Lives," 6.

5. Margaret Guenther, *Holy Listening: The Art of Spiritual Direction* (Boston: Cowley Publications, 1992), 58–61.

GRIEF

1. Roberson, *North Carolina Quilts*, 24–25.

2. Howard E. Friend Jr., *Recovering the Sacred Center: Church Renewal from the Inside Out* (Valley Forge, Pa.: Judson Press, 1998).

JOY

1. Roderick Kiracofe, *Cloth and Comfort* (New York: Clarkson Potter, 1994), 23.

2. Norma Zunich, in interview with South Fork Quilters, Winston-Salem, North Carolina, 1998.

3. Beverly and Gary Young, "In Celebration of Our Anniversary," *The Glass Thimble*, (spring 1999): 3.

4. Wendy Bynner, personal interview, December, 1999.

5. Mary Field Belenky, Blythe McVicker Clinchy, Nancy Rule Goldberger, and Jill Mattuck Tarule, *Women's Ways of Knowing: The Development of Self, Voice, and Mind* (New York: Basic Books, 1986). 48.

6. Henri J. M. Nouwen, *The Genesee Diary: Report from a Trappist Monastery* (New York: Doubleday, 1976), 87.

7. Susan Shie and James Acord of Turtle Moon Studios, in their statement describing "Rainbow Garden," a Green Quilt, 1996.

▪ SELECTED BIBLIOGRAPHY ▪

Belenky, Mary Field, Blythe McVicker Clinchy, Nancy Rule Goldberger, and Jill Mattuck Tarule. *Women's Ways of Knowing: The Development of Self, Voice, and Mind.* 10th ed. New York: Basic Books, 1996.

Benberry, Cuesta. *Always There: The African-American Presence in American Quilts.* Louisville: The Kentucky Quilt Project Inc., 1992.

Bender, Sue. *Everyday Sacred: A Woman's Journey Home.* New York: HarperCollins, 1995.

———. *Plain and Simple: A Woman's Journey to the Amish.* New York: HarperCollins, 1989.

Bole-Becker, Luanne C. *Unraveling the Stories: Quilts as a Reflection of Our Lives.* Cleveland: B. B. Sound & Light Ltd., 1997. Videotape and study guide.

Brackman, Barbara. *Quilts from the Civil War.* Hong Kong: C & T Publishing, 1997.

Bushbaum, Laurie. "Woman of the Cloth." *Art Quilt Magazine,* no. 9 (1998).

Callahan, Nancy. *The Freedom Quilting Bee.* Tuscaloosa: University of Alabama Press, 1987.

Cameron, Julia. *The Artist's Way: A Spiritual Path to Higher Creativity.* New York: G. P. Putnam's Sons, 1992.

Cross, Mary Bywater. *Quilts and Women of the Mormon Migrations.* Nashville: Rutledge Hill Press, 1996.

De Mello, Anthony. *The Song of the Bird.* New York: Doubleday, 1984.

Fellowship of Prayer, A. *The Gift of Prayer: A Treasury of Personal Prayer from the World's Spiritual Traditions.* New York: Continuum, 1995.

Freeman, Roland L. *Communion of the Spirits: African-American Quilters, Preservers, and Their Stories.* Nashville: Rutledge Hill Press, 1996.

Friend, Howard E., Jr. *Recovering the Sacred Center: Church Renewal from the Inside Out.* Valley Forge, Pa.: Judson Press, 1998.

Fry, Gladys-Marie. *Stitched from the Soul: Slave Quilts from the Ante-Bellum South.* New York: Dutton Studio Books, 1990.

Gibeau, Dawn. "Pieces and Patterns of Our Lives." *Praying,* no. 91. Kansas City, Mo.: National Catholic Reporter Publishing Co., Inc. (1 March 1999).

Guenther, Margaret. *Holy Listening: The Art of Spiritual Direction.* Boston: Cowley Publications, 1992.

Hall, Eliza Calvert. *A Quilter's Wisdom.* San Francisco: Chronicle Books, 1994.

Hoffman, Kerry, ed. *Erika Carter: Personal Imagery in Art Quilts.* Bothell, Wash.: Fiber Studio Press and That Patchwork Place, 1996.

Hughes, K. Wind, and Linda Wolf. *Daughters of the Moon, Sisters of the Sun: Young Women and Mentors on the Transition to Womanhood.* British Columbia, Can., and New Haven, Conn.: New Society Publishers, 1997.

Kiracofe, Roderick. *Cloth and Comfort: Pieces of Women's Lives from Their Quilts and Diaries.* New York: Clarkson Potter, 1994.

Lawrence, Kenneth T., ed. *Imaging the Word: An Arts and Lectionary Resource.* Vol. 1. (See also vols. 2 and 3.) Cleveland: United Church Press, 1994.

Lydon, Susan Gordon. *The Knitting Sutra: Craft as a Spiritual Practice.* New York: HarperCollins, 1997.

Mac Dowell, Marsha L. and C. Kurt Dewhurst. *To Honor and Comfort: Native Quilting Traditions.* Santa Fe: Museum of New Mexico Press, 1997.

Magaret, Pat Maixner, and Donna Ingram Slusser. *Watercolor Impressions: Quilts Inspired by the Best Seller Watercolor Quilts.* Bothell, Wash.: That Patchwork Place, 1995.

Mazloomi, Carolyn. *Spirits of the Cloth: Contemporary African-American Quilts.* New York: Clarkson Potter, 1998.

Miller, Margaret J. *Strips that Sizzle.* Bothell, Wash.: That Patchwork Place, 1992.

Nouwen, Henri J. M. *The Genesee Diary: Report from a Trappist Monastery.* New York: Doubleday, 1976.

Roberson, Ruth, ed. *North Carolina Quilts.* Chapel Hill: University of North Carolina Press, 1988.

Root, Elizabeth. *Hawaiian Quilting: Instructions and Full-Size Patterns for 20 Blocks.* New York: Dover Publications, 1989.

Rupp, Joyce. *The Cup of Our Life: A Guide for Spiritual Growth.* Notre Dame, Ind.: Ave Maria Press, 1997.

Salazar, Marie. *The Quilt: Beauty in Fabric and Thread.* New York: Friedman/Fairfax Publishers, 1997.

Scherer, Deidre. *Work in Fabric and Thread.* Lafayette, Calif.: C & T Publishing, 1998.

Serrao, Poakalani and John. *The Hawaiian Quilt: A Spiritual Experience.* Honolulu: Mutual Publishing, 1997.

Simpkinson, Anne, Charles Simpkinson, and Rose Solari, eds. *Nourishing the Soul: Discovering the Sacred in Everyday Life.* San Francisco: Harper San Francisco, 1995.

Taylor, Daphne. "On the American Quilt: Reflections of a Quilter." *Mother Earth News* (December–January 1999).

Thompson, Marjorie. *Soul Feast: An Invitation to the Christian Spiritual Life.* Louisville: Westminster John Knox, 1995.

Tobin, Jacqueline, and Raymond G. Doubard. *Hidden in Plain View: A Secret Story of Quilts and the Underground Railroad.* New York: Doubleday, 1999.

Whitcomb, Holly W. *Feasting with God: Adventures in Table Spirituality.* Cleveland: United Church Press, 1996.

INDEX OF QUILTMAKERS

Other Books from United Church Press and The Pilgrim Press

IN WISDOM'S PATH
Discovering the Sacred in Every Season

Jan L. Richardson

Richardson takes readers on a remarkable journey through the seasons of the church year to discover Wisdom in all her guises. The search takes various forms — striking full-color images, thoughtful and moving prayers, insightful personal reflections — drawn together as a means to help those struggling to find a language that engages us with God, opens us to God, and emerges out of our deepest selves.

0-8298-1324-1/144 pages

Paper/$22.95

WISDOM SEARCHES
Seeking the Feminine Presence of God

Nancy Chinn and Harriet Gleeson

What images and thoughts come to mind as one meditates on the Wisdom literature of the Hebrew and Christian Scriptures? In this devotional book, Nancy Chinn and Harriet Gleeson lead us through their experiences using art, prose, and poetry to guide us to a deeper understanding of Wisdom/Sophia and feminine spirituality.

0-8298-1338-1/128 pages

Cloth/$29.95

PRAYING THE LABYRINTH
A Journey for Spiritual Exploration

Jill Kimberly Hartwell Geoffrion

Foreword by Lauren Artress

Walking the labyrinth is becoming an increasingly popular spiritual exercise across the country and around the world. Based on her experience at Chartes Cathedral in France and her training with Lauren Artress at San Francisco's Grace Cathedral, Jill Geoffrion has created a simple, meaningful approach to preparing for, undertaking, and meditating on labyrinth walks.

0-8298-1343-8/128 pages

Paper/$14.95

LIVING THE LABYRINTH
101 Paths to a Deeper Connection with the Sacred

Jill Kimberly Hartwell Geoffrion

Foreword by Robert Ferré

The follow-up to *Praying the Labyrinth,* Jill Geoffrion takes labyrinth users to the next plateau, encouraging them to expand the ways they approach this unique and ancient spiritual tool.

0-8298-1372-8/104 pages

Paper/$16.95